COMPLETELY UPDATED

FAST FOOD FACTS

Complete Nutrition
Information on More
Than 700 Menu Items
in 15 of the Largest
Fast Food Chains

Marion J. Franz, M.S., R.D., C.D.E.

FOURTH EDITION

**CHRONIMED
PUBLISHING**
Minneapolis, MN

Library of Congress Cataloging-in-Publication Data
Franz, Marion J.
Fast food facts.

1. Convenience foods--Composition--Tables. 2. Food--Composition--Tables. 3. Diabetes--Nutritional aspects. 4. Fast food restaurants--United States.
1. Title
TX551.F74 1993 613.1'8 90-3063
ISBN 0-937721-69-7

Editor: Karol Carstensen
Cover & Text Design: MacLean & Tuminelly
Photography: Paul Lundquist
Production Manager: Claire Lewis
Printed in the United States of America

10 9 8 7 6 5
© 1990, revised 1994
International Diabetes Center

CHRONIMED Publishing
PO Box 47945
Minneapolis, MN 55447-9729

Exchange lists and nutritive values based on *Exchange Lists for Meal Planning* © 1986, American Diabetes Association and The American Dietetic Association.

Table of Contents

Fast Food Tips

by **Marion J. Franz, M.S., R.D., C.D.E**

In a hurry? On the go all the time? Like most Americans, you're probably quite familiar with the fast-food counter or drive-thru at a variety of restaurants. You may be one of the estimated 200 fast-food customers ordering one or more hamburgers every second.

Busy schedules and hectic lifestyles often force people to eat on the run. But we live in an increasingly health-conscious society, and in the last few years we've been hearing more about the perils of fast food. For instance, fast food potentially contributes excess calories, fat, and sodium to the diet and limits important nutrients like calcium, dietary fiber, and vitamins.

Increased consumption of food away from home and increased consumer interest in health, fitness, and nutrition are two seemingly incompatible trends. But don't despair. You *can* eat fast food without sacrificing nutrition or convenience.

For most people, including those with diabetes, an occasional fast-food meal will not upset an otherwise well-balanced diet. What you order and how often you order it are the real issues. Like many lifestyle concerns, moderation is important.

The following tips will help you make the right fast-food choices.

• The keys to nutrition survival are selection and serving size. You need to know your way around a fast-food menu. This book can help you make better food and beverage choices.

• Look for meals that meet these guidelines:

	Men	Women
Calories	800-900	500-600
Fat, grams per meal	30–35	20–25
Sodium, milligrams per meal	<1,000	<1,000

You can easily gulp down half the total number of calories your body needs each day, plus your entire sodium allotment, from a single fast-food meal. If the totals for a meal exceed any of the above, be especially careful in your food choices the rest of the day.

• Eat only at meal times. The average calorie count of a fast-food meal is 685, which is not outrageously high. However, many people eat fast-food items as snacks rather than meals, adding a hefty average of 427 calories to their regular daily intake. That can easily put people well over their daily limits.

• Buy small. Avoid menu choices labeled "jumbo," "giant," or "deluxe." Larger serving sizes mean not only additional calories, but generally more fat, cholesterol, and sodium. Caution is required.

• When ordering burgers, select basic meat items and scale down to single patties. Skip the double burger with cheese or special sauces, especially mayonnaise-based sauces. If you have a double-decker appetite, pile on lettuce and tomatoes instead.

• Battering, breading, or deep-frying cancels out the normal, low-fat advantages of chicken and fish. Choose fish or chicken only if it's unbreaded, and roasted, grilled, or broiled without fat. If fried is your only choice, choose regular coating over extra crispy. Even better, remove the batter and lose calories plus most of the fat and sodium.

• Choose regular or junior sizes of roast beef, ham-and-cheese, and turkey sandwiches. Even with barbecue sauce, a roast beef sandwich will provide fewer calories and be leaner than a hamburger.

• A plain baked potato is nourishing, filling and virtually free of fat and sodium. Adding cheeses, bacon, sour cream, and other toppings can increase the fat level from a trace to 25-30 grams (5 to 6 teaspoons) and the calories from 300 to 600. Top a baked potato with vegetables, one tablespoon of grated cheese (from the salad bar), or 1/4 cup of cottage cheese, and it becomes a complete meal.

• Chili blows the typical "greasy-spoon" reputation. Chili and several restaurant roast beef sandwiches are just about the only fast-food, red-meat dishes that get less than 30% of their calories from fat. Even a large bowl of chili has only 300 calories and 12 grams of fat. Beans are one of the best sources of fiber, making chili and baked beans good choices.

• Pizza, especially cheese pizza topped with mushrooms, green peppers, and onions, can fit nicely into a well-balanced diet as a snack or part of a quick meal. Pepperoni, sausage, anchovies, or extra cheese toppings add unnecessary fat, sodium, and calories. Choosing thin crust over thick also saves calories.

• More and more fast-food restaurants are adding salad bars. A large salad containing a variety of vegetables, 1 cup of cottage cheese, and reduced-calorie salad dressing has less than 250 calories.

• Tacos and tostados are other good calorie and nutrient picks. Go for bean burritos, soft tacos, or other non-fried items. Go easy on the cheese and pass on the sour cream and guacamole. Pile on extra salsa and tomatoes instead.

• Limit salad dressings, mayonnaise, mayonnaise-based sandwich dressings, and other sauces. Each tablespoon of dressing adds an extra 100 to 200 calories to a sandwich or salad.

• Shakes and soft drinks are sources of hidden sugars and fats. Save calories by drinking diet beverages, low-fat milk, fruit juice, or water.

• For dessert bring fresh fruit from home. Or satisfy your sweet tooth with low-fat frozen yogurt or a small ice cream cone.

• If you have fast foods for one meal, try to balance the rest of the day's food choices. Remember, not only is it important to make healthy selections, it's also important to eat all three meals a day, including breakfast and lunch. And don't forget the other side of the equation--exercise.

Today, the health- and calorie-conscious consumer can limit calories, fat, and sodium in fast-food meals. Many fast-food restaurants help by offering salad bars, low-calorie salad dressings, soups, baked potatoes, baked fish, grilled chicken, diet soft drinks, and low-fat milk.

What you are getting in fast foods is often easier to predict than the foods in expensive gourmet restaurants. Fast-foods are remarkably uniform in portion size and nutrition value.

This book is designed to help you make wise food choices by alerting you to the nutritive and exchange values of fast-food items in 16 popular restaurants.

Nutrition Information For 16 Popular Fast-Food Restaurants

Products	SERVING SIZE	CALORIES	CARBO-HYDRATE (gm)

ARBY'S

Sandwiches

Products	SERVING SIZE	CALORIES	CARBO-HYDRATE (gm)
Junior Roast Beef	1 (3.1 oz.)	233	23
Regular Roast Beef	1 (5.5 oz.)	383	35
Beef n Cheddar	1 (7 oz.)	508	43
Bac n Cheddar Deluxe	1 (8 oz.)	512	39
Giant Roast Beef	1 (8.5 oz.)	544	46
Super Roast Beef	1 (9 oz.)	552	54
Philly Beef 'N Swiss	1 (7 oz.)	467	38
French Dip	1 (5.4 oz.)	368	35
French Dip 'N Swiss	1 (6.3 oz.)	429	35
Arby Q	1 (6.7 oz.)	389	48
Chicken Breast Fillet Sandwich	1 (7.2 oz.)	445	42

🗄 = More than 2 fat exchanges per serving

PROTEIN (gm)	FAT (gm)	SAT. FAT (gm)	CHOLES- TEROL (mg)	SODIUM (mg)	Exchanges
12	11	4	22	519	1½ starch, 1½ med. fat meat
22	18	7	43	936	2 starch, 2 med. fat meat, 1½ fat
25	27	8	52	1166	3 starch, 2½ med. fat meat, 2 fat
22	32	8	38	1094	2½ starch, 2 med. fat meat, 4 fat
33	26	11	72	1433	3 starch, 3 med. fat meat, 2 fat
24	28	8	43	1174	3½ starch, 2 med. fat meat, 3 fat
24	25	10	53	1144	2½ starch, 2½ med. fat meat, 2 fat
22	15	6	43	1018	2 starch, 2 med. fat meat, 1 fat
29	19	9	67	1438	2 starch, 3 med. fat meat, 1 fat
18	15	6	29	1268	3 starch, 1 med. fat meat, 2 fat
22	23	3	45	958	3 starch, 2 med. fat meat, 2 fat

♦ = More than 800 milligrams sodium   ♥ = High amounts of sugar

Products	SERVING SIZE	CALORIES	CARBO-HYDRATE (gm)
☥ Roast Chicken Club	1 (8.4 oz.)	503	37
☥ Chicken Cordon Bleu	1 (8 oz.)	518	52
☥ Grilled Chicken Deluxe	1 (8.1 oz.)	430	42
☥ Grilled Chicken Barbeque	1 (7.1 oz.)	386	47
☥ Hot Ham n Cheese Sandwich	1 (6 oz.)	355	35
目 ☥ Fish Fillet Sandwich	1 (7.8 oz.)	526	50
目 ☥ Italian Sub	1 (10.5 oz.)	671	47
☥ Roast Beef Sub	1 (10.8 oz.)	623	47
目 ☥ Tuna Sub	1 (10 oz.)	663	50
☥ Turkey Sub	1 (9.7 oz.)	486	46

Light Menu

Light Roast Chicken Deluxe	1 (6.8 oz.)	276	33
☥ Light Roast Turkey Deluxe	1 (6.8 oz.)	260	33

目 = More than 2 fat exchanges per serving

PROTEIN (gm)	FAT (gm)	SAT. FAT (gm)	CHOLES- TEROL (mg)	SODIUM (mg)	Exchanges
30	27	7	46	1143	2½ starch, 3 med. fat meat, 2 fat
30	27	5	92	1463	3 starch, 3 med. fat meat, 2 fat
24	20	4	44	901	2½ starch, 2½ med. fat meat, 1 fat
24	13	4	43	1002	3 starch, 2 med. fat meat
25	14	5	55	1400	2 starch, 3 med. fat meat
23	27	7	44	872	3 starch, 2 med. fat meat, 3 fat
34	39	13	69	2062	3 starch, 3½ med. fat meat, 4 fat
38	32	12	73	1847	3 starch, 4 med. fat meat, 2 fat
34	37	8	43	1342	3 starch, 3½ med. fat meat, 4 fat
33	19	5	51	2033	3 starch, 3½ med. fat meat
24	7	2	33	777	2 starch, 2½ lean meat
20	6	2	33	1262	2 starch, 2 lean meat

☂ = More than 800 milligrams sodium   ♣ = High amounts of sugar

Products	SERVING SIZE	CALORIES	CARBO-HYDRATE (gm)
Light Roast Beef Deluxe	1 (6.4 oz.)	294	33
Potatoes			
Baked Potato, Plain	1 (8.5 oz.)	240	50
▤ Baked Potato, with Butter, Sour Cream	1 (11 oz.)	463	53
▤ Broccoli 'N Cheddar Baked Potato	1 (12 oz.)	417	55
▤ Deluxe Baked Potato	1 (12.3 oz.)	621	59
▤ ☀ Mushroom 'N Cheese Baked Potato	1 (12.3 oz.)	515	58
French Fries	1 (2.5 oz.)	246	30
Potato Cakes	1 (3 oz.)	204	20
▤ Curly Fries	1 (3.5 oz.)	337	43
▤ Cheddar Fries	1 (5 oz.)	399	46
Salads			
Garden Salad	1 (11.6 oz.)	117	11

▤ = More than 2 fat exchanges per serving

PROTEIN (gm)	FAT (gm)	SAT. FAT (gm)	CHOLES-TEROL (mg)	SODIUM (mg)	Exchanges
18	10	4	42	826	2 starch, 2 med. meat
6	2	0	0	58	3 starch
8	25	12	40	203	3 starch, 5 fat
11	18	7	22	361	3 starch 1 vegetable, 1 high fat meat, 2 fat
17	36	18	58	605	4 starch, 1 high fat meat, 5 fat
15	27	6	47	923	4 starch, 1 high fat meat, 3 fat
2	13	3	0	114	2 starch, 2 fat
2	12	2	0	397	1½ starch, 2 fat
4	18	7	0	167	3 starch, 3 fat
6	22	9	9	443	3 starch, 4 fat
7	5	3	12	134	2 vegetable 1 fat

☂ = More than 800 milligrams sodium   ♣ = High amounts of sugar

Products	SERVING SIZE	CALORIES	CARBO-HYDRATE (gm)
Roast Chicken Salad	1 (14 oz.)	204	24
Chef Salad	1 (14.5 oz.)	205	13
Side Salad	1 (5.3 oz.)	25	4

Salad Dressings/Condiments

	Products	SERVING SIZE	CALORIES	CARBO-HYDRATE (gm)
ᗺ	Honey French Dressing	1 (2 oz.)	322	22
⚕	Light Italian Dressing	1 (2 oz.)	23	3
ᗺ	Thousand Island Dressing	1 (2 oz.)	298	10
ᗺ	Blue Cheese Dressing	1 (2 oz.)	295	2
ᗺ	Buttermilk Ranch Dressing	1 (2 oz.)	349	2
	Croutons	1 (.5 oz.)	59	8
	Arby's Sauce	1 (.5 oz.)	15	3
	Horsey Sauce	1 (.5 oz.)	55	3
	Ketchup	1 (.5 oz.)	16	4
	Mustard	1 (.5 oz.)	11	tr
	Mayonnaise P.C.	1 (.5 oz.)	90	0

ᗺ = More than 2 fat exchanges per serving

PROTEIN (gm)	FAT (gm)	SAT. FAT (gm)	CHOLES-TEROL (mg)	SODIUM (mg)	Exchanges
12	7	3	43	508	1 starch, 2 vegetable, 1 med. fat meat
19	10	4	126	796	2 vegetable 2 med. fat meat
2	tr	-	0	30	1 vegetable
tr	27	4	0	486	1 starch, 5 fat
0	1	-	0	1110	Free
tr	29	4	24	493	½ starch 6 fat
2	31	6	50	489	6 fat
tr	39	6	6	471	8 fat
2	2	tr	1	155	½ starch
tr	tr	0	113		Free
tr	5	-	105		1 fat
tr	0	0	0	143	Free
tr	tr	0	0	160	Free
0	10	1	0	75	2 fat

🍴 = More than 800 milligrams sodium   ♥ = High amounts of sugar

Products	SERVING SIZE	CALORIES	CARBO-HYDRATE (gm)
Soups			
ⵌ Boston Clam Chowder	1 (8 oz.)	193	18
ⵌ Cream of Broccoli Soup	1 (8 oz.)	166	18
ⵌ Lumberjack Mixed Vegetable Soup	1 (8 oz.)	89	13
ⵌ Old Fashioned Chicken Noodle	1 (8 oz.)	99	15
ⵌ Potato with Bacon Soup	1 (8 oz.)	184	20
ⵌ Wisconsin Cheese Soup	1 (8 oz.)	281	20
Breakfast Items			
⾐ Toastix	1 (3.5 oz.)	420	43
ⵖ Maple Syrup	1 (1.5 oz.)	120	29
Cinnamon Nut Danish	1 (3.5 oz.)	360	60
⾐ Plain Biscuit	1 (2.9 oz.)	280	34
⾐ⵌ Bacon Biscuit	1 (3.1 oz.)	318	35

⾐ = More than 2 fat exchanges per serving

PROTEIN (gm)	FAT (gm)	SAT. FAT (gm)	CHOLES- TEROL (mg)	SODIUM (mg)	Exchanges
8	10	5	26	1032	1 starch, 2 fat
8	7	4	24	1050	1 starch, 2 fat
2	3	2	4	1075	1 starch
6	2	-	25	929	1 starch
6	9	4	20	1068	1 starch, 2 fat
9	18	9	32	1084	1 starch, 1 high fat meat, 2 fat
8	25	5	20	440	3 starch, 4 fat
0	tr	0	0	52	2 starch or 2 fruit
6	11	1	0	105	4 starch 2 fat
6	15	3	0	730	2 starch 3 fat
7	18	5	8	904	2 starch 4 fat

☧ = More than 800 milligrams sodium   ♥ = High amounts of sugar

	Products	SERVING SIZE	CALORIES	CARBO-HYDRATE (gm)
🅱🇹	Sausage Biscuit	1 (4.2 oz.)	460	35
🇹	Ham Biscuit	1 (4.4 oz.)	323	34
🅱	Plain Croissant	1 (2.2)	260	28
🅱	Bacon/Egg Croissant	1 (4.3 oz.)	430	29
🇹	Ham/Cheese Croissant	1 (4.2 oz.)	345	29
🅱🇹	Mushroom/Cheese Croissant	1 (5.2 oz.)	493	34
🅱🇹	Sausage/Egg Croissant	1 (5 oz.)	519	29
🅱🇹	Ham Platter	1 (9.1 oz.)	518	45
🅱🇹	Sausage Platter	1 (8.4 oz.)	640	46
🅱	Egg Platter	1 (7.1 oz.)	460	45
🅱🇹	Bacon Platter	1 (7.8 oz.)	593	51
	Blueberry Muffin	1 (2.7 oz.)	240	40
	Orange Juice	1 (6 oz.)	82	20

🅱 = More than 2 fat exchanges per serving

PROTEIN (gm)	FAT (gm)	SAT. FAT (gm)	CHOLES-TEROL (mg)	SODIUM (mg)	Exchanges
12	32	10	60	1000	2 starch, 1 high fat meat, 5 fat
13	17	4	21	1169	2 starch, 1 med. fat meat. 2 fat
6	16	10	49	300	2 starch, 3 fat
17	30	15	245	720	2 starch, 2 med. fat meat, 3 fat
16	21	12	90	939	2 starch, 1½ med. fat meat, 2 fat
13	38	15	116	935	2 starch, 1 med. fat meat, 6 fat
18	39	19	271	632	2 starch, 2 med. fat meat, 5 fat
24	26	8	374	1177	3 starch, 2 med. fat meat, 3 fat
21	41	13	406	861	3 starch, 2 med. fat meat, 6 fat
15	24	7	346	591	3 starch, 1 med. fat meat, 4 fat
22	33	9	458	880	3½ starch, 2 med. fat meat, 4 fat
4	7	1	22	200	2½ starch, 1 fat
1	0	0	0	2	1 fruit

🛉 = More than 800 milligrams sodium   ♥ = High amounts of sugar

Products	SERVING SIZE	CALORIES	CARBO-HYDRATE (gm)
♥ Hot Chocolate	1 (8 oz.)	110	23

OCCASIONAL USE

Products	SERVING SIZE	CALORIES	CARBO-HYDRATE (gm)
目 ♥ Apple Turnover	1 (3 oz.)	303	28
目 ♥ Cherry Turnover	1 (3 oz.)	280	25
目 ♥ Blueberry Turnover	1 (3 oz.)	320	32
目 ♥ Cheese Cake	1 (3 oz.)	306	21
Chocolate Chip Cookie	1 (1 oz.)	130	17
♥ Vanilla Shake	1 (11 oz.)	330	46

NOT RECOMMENDED FOR USE

Products	SERVING SIZE	CALORIES	CARBO-HYDRATE (gm)
♥ Chocolate Shake	1 (12 oz.)	451	76
♥ Jamocha Shake	1 (11.5 oz.)	368	59
目 ♥ Peanut Butter Cup Polar Swirl	1 (11.6 oz.)	517	61
目 ♥ Oreo Polar Swirl	1 (11.6 oz.)	482	66
目 ♥ Snickers Polar Swirl	1 (11.6 oz.)	511	73

目 = More than 2 fat exchanges per serving

PROTEIN (gm)	FAT (gm)	SAT. FAT (gm)	CHOLES-TEROL (mg)	SODIUM (mg)	Exchanges
2	1	tr	0	120	1½ starch
4	18	7	0	178	2 starch, 3 fat
4	18	5	0	200	2 starch, 3 fat
3	19	6	0	240	2 starch, 3½ fat
5	23	7	95	220	1½ starch, 4 fat
2	4	2	0	95	1 starch, 1 fat
11	12	4	32	281	3 starch, 2 fat
10	12	3	36	341	
9	11	3	35	262	
14	24	8	34	386	
11	20	10	35	521	
12	19	7	33	351	

⌀ = More than 800 milligrams sodium   ♥ = High amounts of sugar

Products	SERVING SIZE	CALORIES	CARBO-HYDRATE (gm)
🅱🛒 Heath Polar Swirl	1 (11.6 oz.)	543	76
🅱🛒 Butterfinger Polar	1 (11.6 oz.)	457	62

BURGER KING

Sandwiches

Products	SERVING SIZE	CALORIES	CARBO-HYDRATE (gm)
Hamburger	1 (3.6 oz.)	260	28
Cheeseburger	1 (4 oz.)	300	28
🅱🎋 Whopper Sandwich	1 (9.5 oz.)	570	46
🅱🎋 Whopper w/Cheese	1 (10.3 oz.)	660	48
Whopper Jr.	1 (4.7 oz.)	300	29
Whopper Jr. w/Cheese	1 (5 oz.)	350	30
🅱🎋 Double Whopper	1 (12.3 oz.)	800	46
🅱🎋 Double Whopper with Cheese	1 (13.2 oz.)	890	48

🅱 = More than 2 fat exchanges per serving

PROTEIN (gm)	FAT (gm)	SAT. FAT (gm)	CHOLES-TEROL (mg)	SODIUM (mg)	Exchanges
11	22	5	39	346	
12	18	8	28	318	
14	10	4	30	500	2 starch, 2 med. fat meat
16	14	6	45	660	2 starch, 2 med. fat meat, 1 fat
27	31	12	80	870	3 starch, 3 med. fat meat, 3 fat
32	38	14	105	1190	3 starch, 4 med. fat meat, 3 fat
14	15	5	35	500	2 starch, 1½ med. fat meat, 1 fat
16	19	7	45	650	2 starch, 2 med. fat meat, 1 fat
46	48	18	160	940	3 starch, 5 med. fat meat, 4 fat
51	55	22	185	1250	3 starch, 6 med. fat meat, 5 fat

🍴 = More than 800 milligrams sodium   🍬 = High amounts of sugar

Products	SERVING SIZE	CALORIES	CARBO-HYDRATE (gm)
ⵟ Bacon Double Cheeseburger	1 (5.3 oz.)	470	26
ⵗ ⵟ Bacon Double Cheeseburger Deluxe	1 (6.5 oz.)	530	28
ⵟ Double Cheeseburger	1 (5.6 oz.)	450	29
BK Broiler Chicken Sandwich	1 (5.4 oz.)	280	29
ⵗ ⵟ Chicken Sandwich	1 (8 oz.)	620	57
Chicken Tenders	6 pieces	236	14
ⵗ Ocean Catch Fish Filet Sandwich	1 (5.8 oz.)	450	33

Side Orders

Products	SERVING SIZE	CALORIES	CARBO-HYDRATE (gm)
Chef Salad w/out Salad Dressing	1 (9.6 oz.)	178	7
Chicken Salad w/out Salad Dressing	1 (9 oz.)	142	8
Garden Salad w/out Salad Dressing	1 (7.8 oz.)	95	8
Side Salad w/out Salad Dressing	1 (4.8 oz.)	25	5

ⵗ = More than 2 fat exchanges per serving

PROTEIN (gm)	FAT (gm)	SAT. FAT (gm)	CHOLES-TEROL (mg)	SODIUM (mg)	Exchanges
30	28	13	100	800	2 starch, 3 med. fat meat, 2 fat
30	33	14	100	860	2 starch, 3 med. fat meat, 3 fat
27	25	12	90	840	2 starch, 3 med. fat meat, 2 fat
20	10	2	50	770	2 starch, 2 med. fat meat
26	32	7	45	1430	4 starch, 2 med. fat meat, 4 fat
16	13	3	38	541	1 starch, 2 med. fat meat
16	28	7	30	760	2 starch, 2 med. fat meat, 3 fat
17	9	4	103	568	1 vegetable, 2 med. fat meat
20	4	1	49	443	1 vegetable, 2 lean meat
6	5	3	15	125	1 vegetable, 1 med. fat meat
1	0	0	0	27	1 vegetable

☂ = More than 800 milligrams sodium   ♥ =·High amounts of sugar

Products	SERVING SIZE	CALORIES	CARBO-HYDRATE (gm)
▐ Onion Rings	1 (3.4 oz.)	339	38
▐ French Fries (medium, salted)	1 (4 oz.)	372	43

Salad Dressings/Condiments

BK Broiler Sauce	1 (.4 oz.)	37	1
Bull's Eye Barbecue Sauce	1 (.5 oz.)	22	5
▐ Mayonnaise Reduced Calorie	1 (1 oz.)	130	3
Tartar Sauce	1 (1 oz.)	100	4
▐ Thousand Island Dressing	1 (2.2 oz.)	290	15
▐ Blue Cheese Salad Dressing	1 (2 oz.)	300	2
▐ French Dressing	1 (2.2 oz.)	290	23
▐ Ranch Dressing	1 (2 oz.)	350	4
Light Italian Dressing	1 (2 oz.)	30	6
A.M. Express Dip	1 (1 oz.)	84	21
Honey Dipping Sauce	1 (1 oz.)	91	23
▐ Ranch Dipping Sauce	1 (1 oz.)	171	2

▐ = More than 2 fat exchanges per serving

PROTEIN (gm)	FAT (gm)	SAT. FAT (gm)	CHOLES- TEROL (mg)	SODIUM (mg)	Exchanges
5	19	5	0	628	2½ starch, 3 fat
5	20	5	0	238	3 starch, 3 fat
0	4	1	5	74	1 fat
0	0	0	0	47	Free
0	13	2	0	150	2½ fat
0	10	2	0	220	2 fat
1	26	5	36	403	1 starch, 5 fat
3	32	7	58	512	6 fat
0	22	3	0	400	1 starch, 5 fat
1	37	7	20	316	8 fat
0	1	0	0	710	½ fat
0	0	0	0	18	1 starch
0	0	0	0	12	1½ starch
0	18	3	0	208	4 fat

🛆 = More than 800 milligrams sodium   ♥ = High amounts of sugar

Products	SERVING SIZE	CALORIES	CARBO-HYDRATE (gm)
Barbecue Sauce	1 (1 oz.)	36	9
Sweet & Sour Dipping Sauce	1 (1 oz.)	45	11

Breakfast Items

▤ Bacon, Egg, Cheese Croissanwich	1 (4 oz.)	353	19
▤ ☀ Sausage, Egg, Cheese Croissanwich	1 (5.6 oz.)	534	22
☀ Ham, Egg, Cheese Croissanwich	1 (5 oz.)	351	20
Breakfast Buddy with Sausage, Egg, Cheese	1 (3 oz.)	255	15
▤ French Toast Sticks	1 (5 oz.)	440	60
Hash Browns	1 (2.5 oz.)	213	25
Blueberry Mini Muffins	1 (3.3 oz.)	292	37
Orange Juice	1 (6.5 oz.)	82	20

OCCASIONAL USE

�099 Apple Pie	1 (4.5 oz.)	320	45

▤ = More than 2 fat exchanges per serving

PROTEIN (gm)	FAT (gm)	SAT. FAT (gm)	CHOLES-TEROL (mg)	SODIUM (mg)	Exchanges
0	0	0	0	397	½ starch
0	0	0	0	52	½ starch
16	23	8	230	780	1 starch, 2 med. fat meat, 3 fat
21	40	14	258	985	1½ starch, 2½ med. fat meat, 5 fat
19	22	7	236	1373	1½ starch, 2 med. fat meat, 2 fat
11	16	6	127	492	1 starch, 1 med. fat meat, 2 fat
4	27	7	0	490	4 starch, 4 fat
2	12	3	0	318	1½ starch, 2 fat
4	14	3	72	244	2½ starch, 2 fat
1	0	0	0	2	1½ fruit
3	14	4	0	420	2 starch, 1 fruit, 2 fat

☂ = More than 800 milligrams sodium   ♥ = High amounts of sugar

	Products	SERVING SIZE	CALORIES	CARBO-HYDRATE (gm)
♥	Cherry Pie	1 (4.5 oz.)	360	55
♥	Lemon Pie	1 (3.2 oz.)	290	49
目 ♥	Snickers Ice Cream Bar	1 (2 oz.)	220	20
♥	Vanilla Shake	1 (10 oz.)	334	51
♥	Chocolate Shake	1 (10 oz.)	326	49

NOT RECOMMENDED FOR USE

♥	Chocolate Shake (syrup added)	1 (11 oz.)	409	68
♥	Strawberry Shake (syrup added)	1 (11 oz.)	394	66

CHURCH'S FRIED CHICKEN

Chicken

Fried Chicken Breast	1 (2.8 oz.)	200	4
Wing	1 (3.1 oz.)	250	8
Thigh	1 (2.8 oz.)	230	5
Leg	1 (2 oz.)	140	2

目 = More than 2 fat exchanges per serving

PROTEIN (gm)	FAT (gm)	SAT. FAT (gm)	CHOLES-TEROL (mg)	SODIUM (mg)	Exchanges
4	13	4	0	200	2½ starch, 1 fruit, 2 fat
6	8	3	35	105	3 starch, 1 fat
5	14	7	15	65	1½ starch, 2½ fat
9	10	6	33	213	3 starch, 2 fat
9	10	6	31	198	3 starch, 2 fat
10	11	6	33	248	
9	10	6	33	230	
19	12	NA	65	510	3 med. fat meat
19	16	NA	60	540	½ starch, 2 med. fat meat, 1 fat
16	16	NA	80	520	2 med. fat meat, 1 fat
13	9	NA	45	160	2 med. fat meat

☂ = More than 800 milligrams sodium   ♥ = High amounts of sugar

Products	SERVING SIZE	CALORIES	CARBO-HYDRATE (gm)
Accompaniments			
Cajun Rice	3.1 oz.	130	16
Potatoes & Gravy	3.7 oz.	90	14
Corn on the Cob	5.7 oz.	190	32
French Fries	2.7 oz.	210	29
Okra	2.8 oz.	210	19
Biscuits	2.1 oz.	250	26
Cole Slaw	3 oz.	92	8
OCCASIONAL USE			
♥ Apple Pie	3.1 oz.	280	41

DAIRY QUEEN

Sandwiches

Single Hamburger	1 (5 oz.)	310	29
Double Hamburger	1 (7 oz.)	460	29
Single w/Cheese	1 (5.5 oz.)	365	30

目 = More than 2 fat exchanges per serving

PROTEIN (gm)	FAT (gm)	SAT. FAT (gm)	CHOLES- TEROL (mg)	SODIUM (mg)	Exchanges
1	7	NA	5	260	1 starch, 1 fat
1	3	NA	0	520	1 starch
8	5	NA	0	15	2 starch, 1 fat
3	11	NA	0	605	2 starch, 2 fat
3	16	NA	0	520	1 starch, 3 fat
2	16	NA	5	640	2 starch, 2 fat
4	6	NA	0	230	1 vegetable, 1 fat
2	12	NA	5	340	2 starch, 1 fruit 2 fat
17	13	6	45	580	2 starch, 2 med. fat meat
31	25	12	95	630	2 starch, 4 med. fat meat
20	18	9	60	800	2 starch, 2 med. fat meat, 1 fat

⌀ = More than 800 milligrams sodium   ♥ = High amounts of sugar

Products	SERVING SIZE	CALORIES	CARBO-HYDRATE (gm)
✝ Double w/Cheese	1 (8 oz.)	570	31
🅱 ✝ DQ Homestyle Ultimate Burger	1 (9.7 oz.)	700	30
Hot Dog	1 (3.5 oz.)	280	23
🅱 Hot Dog w/Chili	1 (4.5 oz.)	320	26
🅱 ✝ Hot Dog w/Cheese	1 (4 oz.)	330	24
🅱 ✝ Quarter Pound Super Dog	1 (7 oz.)	590	41
BBQ Beef Sandwich	1 (4.5 oz.)	225	34
Fish Fillet Sandwich	1 (6 oz.)	370	39
✝ Fish Fillet w/Cheese	1 (6.5 oz.)	420	40
Grilled Chicken Fillet Sandwich	1 (6.5 oz.)	300	33
Breaded Chicken Fillet Sandwich	1 (6.7 oz.)	430	37
✝ Breaded Chicken Fillet w/Cheese	1 (7.2 oz.)	480	38

🅱 = More than 2 fat exchanges per serving

PROTEIN (gm)	FAT (gm)	SAT. FAT (gm)	CHOLES-TEROL (mg)	SODIUM (mg)	Exchanges
37	34	18	120	1070	2 starch, 4½ med. fat meat, 2 fat
43	47	21	140	1110	2 starch, 5 med. fat meat, 4 fat
9	16	6	25	700	1½ starch, 1 med. fat meat, 2 fat
11	19	7	30	720	1½ starch, 1 med. fat meat, 3 fat
12	21	9	55	920	1½ starch, 1 med. fat meat, 3 fat
20	38	16	60	1360	3 starch, 2 med. fat meat, 5 fat
12	4	1	20	700	2 starch, 1 med. fat meat
16	16	3	45	630	2½ starch, 1 med. fat meat, 2 fat
19	21	7	60	850	2½ starch, 2 med. fat meat, 2 fat
25	8	2	50	800	2 starch, 3 lean meat
24	20	4	55	760	2½ starch, 2½ med. fat meat, 1 fat
27	25	7	70	980	2½ starch, 3 med. fat meat, 2 fat

☂ = More than 800 milligrams sodium   ♣ = High amounts of sugar

Products	SERVING SIZE	CALORIES	CARBO- HYDRATE (gm)
Side Orders			
French Fries	Small	210	29
French Fries	Regular	300	40
▉ French Fries	Large	390	52
Onion Rings	1 (3 oz.)	240	29
Side Salad without Dressing	1 (4.8 oz.)	25	4
Garden Salad without Dressing	1 (10 oz.)	200	7
▉ Thousand Island Dressing	2 oz.	225	10
Reduced Calorie French Dressing	2 oz.	90	11
Lettuce	.5 oz.	2	0
Tomato	.5 oz.	3	0
OCCASIONAL USE			
♥ Vanilla Cone	Small	140	22
♥ Vanilla Cone	Regular	230	36
♥ Vanilla Cone	Large	340	53
♥ Chocolate Cone	Regular	230	36
♥ Chocolate Cone	Large	350	54

▉ = More than 2 fat exchanges per serving

PROTEIN (gm)	FAT (gm)	SAT. FAT (gm)	CHOLES-TEROL (mg)	SODIUM (mg)	Exchanges
3	10	2	0	115	1½ starch, 2 fat
4	14	3	0	160	2½ starch, 2½ fat
5	18	4	0	200	3½ starch, 3 fat
4	12	3	0	135	2 starch, 2 fat
1	0	0	0	15	1 vegetable
13	13	7	185	240	1 vegetable, 2 med. fat meat, 1 fat
tr	21	3	25	570	½ starch, 4 fat
tr	5	1	0	450	½ starch, 1 fat
0	0	0	0	1	Free
0	0	0	0	1	Free
4	4	3	15	60	1½ starch, 1 fat
6	7	5	20	95	2½ starch, 1 fat
8	10	7	30	140	3½ starch, 1½ fat
6	7	5	20	115	2½ fat, 1 fat
8	11	8	30	170	3½ starch, 1½ fat

� = More than 800 milligrams sodium   ' ♥ = High amounts of sugar

Products	SERVING SIZE	CALORIES	CARBO-HYDRATE (gm)
▤ ♥ Chocolate Dipped Cone	Regular	330	40
♥ Chocolate Sundae	Regular	300	54
♥ Strawberry Waffle Cone Sundae	1 (6 oz.)	350	56
♥ DQ Sandwich	1 (2 oz.)	140	24
♥ Dilly Bar	1 (3 oz.)	210	21
♥ Mr. Misty	Regular	250	63
♥ Yogurt Cone	Regular	180	38
♥ Yogurt Cone	Large	260	56
♥ Cup of Yogurt	Regular	170	35
♥ Cup of Yogurt	Large	230	49
♥ Yogurt Strawberry Sundae	Regular	200	43
♥ Strawberry Breeze	Small	290	63
▤ ♥ QC Vanilla Big Scoop	1 (4.5 oz.)	300	39
▤ ♥ QC Chocolate Big Scoope	1 (4.5 oz.)	310	40

NOT RECOMMENDED FOR USE

▤ ♥ Vanilla Shake	Regular	520	88

▤ = More than 2 fat exchanges per serving

PROTEIN (gm)	FAT (gm)	SAT. FAT (gm)	CHOLES-TEROL (mg)	SODIUM (mg)	Exchanges
6	16	8	20	100	2½ starch, 3 fat
6	7	5	20	140	3½ starch, 1 fat
8	12	5	20	220	3½ starch, 2 fat
3	4	2	5	135	1½ starch, 1 fat
3	13	6	10	50	1½ starch, 2 fat
0	0	0	0	0	4 fruit
6	tr	tr	tr	80	2½ starch
9	tr	tr	5	115	3½ starch
6	tr	tr	tr	70	2 starch
8	tr	tr	tr	100	3 starch
6	tr	tr	tr	80	2 starch, 1 fruit
9	tr	tr	5	115	4 starch
5	14	9	35	100	2½ starch, 2½ fat
5	14	10	35	100	2½ starch, 2½ fat
12	14	8	45	230	

☎ = More than 800 milligrams sodium   ♥ = High amounts of sugar

Products	SERVING SIZE	CALORIES	CARBO-HYDRATE (gm)
🦷🦷 Vanilla Shake	Large	600	101
🦷🦷 Chocolate Shake	Regular	540	94
🦷🦷 Vanilla Malt	Regular	610	106
🦷 Banana Split	1 (13 oz.)	510	93
🦷🦷 Peanut Buster Parfait	1 10.8 oz.)	710	94
🦷🦷 Hot Fudge Brownie Delight	1 (10.8 oz.)	710	102
🦷🦷 Nutty Double Fudge	(9.7 oz.)	580	85
🦷🦷 Buster Bar	1 5.25 oz.)	450	40
🦷 Strawberry Blizzard	Small	400	64
🦷🦷 Strawberry Blizzard	Regular	570	92
🦷🦷 Heath Blizzard	Small	560	79
🦷🦷 Heath Blizzard	Regular	820	114
🦷🦷 DQ Frozen Cake	1 (5.8 oz.)	380	50

🦷 = More than 2 fat exchanges per serving

PROTEIN (gm)	FAT (gm)	SAT. FAT (gm)	CHOLES- TEROL (mg)	SODIUM (mg)	Exchanges
13	16	10	50	260	
12	14	8	45	290	
13	14	8	45	230	
9	11	8	30	250	
16	32	10	30	410	
11	29	14	35	340	
10	22	10	35	170	
11	29	9	15	220	
9	12	8	35	160	
13	16	11	50	230	
11	23	11	40	280	
16	36	17	60	410	
6	18	8	20	210	

� = More than 800 milligrams sodium   ♥ = High amounts of sugar

Products	SERVING SIZE	CALORIES	CARBO-HYDRATE (gm)
♥ Strawberry Breeze	Regular	420	90
♥ Heath Breeze	Small	450	78
目 ♥ Heath Breeze	Regular	680	113

DOMINO'S PIZZA

Pizza

Cheese Pizza 16" (large)	2 slices (5.5 oz.)	376	56
✝ Pepperoni Pizza 16" (large)	2 slices (5.5 oz.)	460	56
Sausage/Mushroom Pizza 16" (large)	2 slices (5.5 oz.)	430	55
✝ Veggie Pizza 16" (large) includes mushrooms, onion, green pepper, double cheese, olives	2 slices (5.5 oz.)	498	60
✝ Deluxe Pizza 16" (large) includes sausage, pepperoni, onion, green pepper, mushrooms	2 slices (5.5 oz.)	498	59
✝ Double Cheese/ Pepperoni Pizza 16" (large)	2 slices (5.5 oz.)	545	55

目 = More than 2 fat exchanges per serving

PROTEIN (gm)	FAT (gm)	SAT. FAT (gm)	CHOLES- TEROL (mg)	SODIUM (mg)	Exchanges
12	1	tr	5	170	
11	12	3	10	230	
15	21	6	15	360	
22	10	6	19	483	4 starch, 2 med. fat meat
24	18	9	28	825	4 starch, 2 med. fat meat, 2 fat
24	16	8	28	552	4 starch, 2 med. fat meat, 1 fat
31	19	10	36	1035	4 starch, 3 med. fat meat, 1 fat
27	20	9	40	954	4 starch, 2 med. fat meat, 2 fat
32	25	13	48	1042	4 starch, 3 med. fat meat, 2 fat

☂ = More than 800 milligrams sodium   ♥ = High amounts of sugar

Products	SERVING SIZE	CALORIES	CARBO-HYDRATE (gm)
✝ Ham Pizza 16" (large)	2 slices (5.5 oz.)	417	58

HARDEE'S

Sandwiches/Subs

Hamburger	1 (3.5 oz.)	260	33
Cheeseburger	1 (4.3 oz.)	300	34
目 ✝ Quarter-Pound Cheeseburger	1 (6.4 oz.)	500	34
目 ✝ Big Deluxe Burger	1 (7.6 oz.)	500	32
目 ✝ Bacon Cheeseburger	1 (7.7 oz.)	610	31
✝ Mushroom N Swiss Burger	1 (6.5 oz.)	490	33
目 ✝ Frisco Burger	1 (8.5 oz.)	760	43
目 ✝ Real West Bacon & Cheese Burger	1 (7.6 oz.)	560	38
目 ✝ New York Patty Melt	1 (8.5 oz.)	780	45

目 = More than 2 fat exchanges per serving

PROTEIN (gm)	FAT (gm)	SAT. FAT (gm)	CHOLES-TEROL (mg)	SODIUM (mg)	Exchanges
23	11	6	26	805	4 starch, 2 med. fat meat
10	10	4	30	510	2 starch, 1 med. fat meat, 1 fat
12	14	6	40	740	2 starch, 1 med. fat meat, 2 fat
29	29	14	70	1060	2 starch, 3 med. fat meat, 3 fat
27	30	12	70	760	2 starch, 3 med. fat meat, 3 fat
34	39	16	80	1030	2 starch, 4 med. fat meat, 3 fat
30	27	13	70	940	2 starch, 3½ med. fat meat, 2 fat
36	50	18	70	1280	3 starch, 4 med. fat meat, 5 fat
33	31	14	45	1130	2½ starch, 3½ med. fat meat, 2½ fat
35	51	20	80	990	3 starch, 3½ med. fat meat, 6 fat

Ⓧ = More than 800 milligrams sodium   ♥ = High amounts of sugar

Products	SERVING SIZE	CALORIES	CARBO-HYDRATE (gm)
☂ Roast Beef Sandwich	Regular (4 oz.)	280	29
☂ Big Roast Beef Sandwich	1 (4.7 oz.)	380	29
☂ Real West BBQ Beef Sandwich	1 7 oz.	350	48
☂ Hot Ham N Cheese	1 (5.25 oz.)	330	32
☂ Fisherman's Fillet	1 (7.5 oz.)	480	50
☂ Turkey Club	1 (7.3 oz.)	390	32
𝕭 ☂ Frisco Club	1 (8.5 oz.)	620	46
☂ Chicken Fillet	1 (6 oz.)	370	44
𝕭 ☂ Frisco Chicken	1 (8.6 oz.)	620	44
☂ Grilled Chicken Breast Sandwich	1 ((6.8 oz.)	310	34
Big Twin	1 (6 oz.)	450	34
☂ Reuben Sandwich	1 (9.3 oz.)	540	48

𝕭 = More than 2 fat exchanges per serving

PROTEIN (gm)	FAT (gm)	SAT. FAT (gm)	CHOLES- TEROL (mg)	SODIUM (mg)	Exchanges
18	11	4	40	870	2 starch, 2 med. fat meat
26	18	8	60	1230	2 starch, 3 med. fat meat
18	9	4	36	1290	3 starch, 1 med. fat meat, 1 fat
23	12	5	65	1420	2 starch, 2½ med. fat meat
23	21	6	70	1210	3 starch, 2 med. fat meat, 2 fat
29	16	4	70	1280	2 starch, 3 med. fat meat
30	35	11	75	1930	3 starch, 3 med. fat meat, 4 fat
19	13	2	55	1060	3 starch, 2 med. fat meat
35	34	10	95	1730	3 starch, 3½ med. fat meat, 3 fat
24	9	1	60	890	2 starch, 2½ lean meat
23	25	11	55	580	2 starch, 3 med. fat meat, 2 fat
35	22	6	80	1610	3 starch, 4 med. fat meat

☛ = More than 800 milligrams sodium   ♥ = High amounts of sugar

	Products	SERVING SIZE	CALORIES	CARBO-HYDRATE (gm)
	Hot Dog	1 (4 oz.)	290	26
*	Turkey Sub	1 ((9.3 oz.)	390	53
*	Roast Beef Sub	1 ((9 oz.)	370	57
*	Ham Sub	1 ((8.6 oz.)	370	52
*	Combo Sub	1 ((9 oz.)	380	52
	Fried Chicken Breast	1 (4 oz.)	340	15
	Wing	(2 oz.)	205	9
	Thigh	1 (3.8 oz.)	370	13
	Leg	1 (2 oz.)	152	6
	Chicken Stix	6 Pieces (3.5 oz.)	210	13
*	Chicken Stix	9 Pieces (5.3 oz.)	310	20

■ = More than 2 fat exchanges per serving

PROTEIN (gm)	FAT (gm)	SAT. FAT (gm)	CHOLES-TEROL (mg)	SODIUM (mg)	Exchanges
11	16	4	30	760	2 starch, 1 high fat meat, 1 fat
29	7	4	65	1420	3½ starch, 2½ lean meat
23	5	3	45	1400	3½ starch, 2 lean meat
25	7	4	45	1400	3½ starch, 2 lean meat
28	6	3	45	1440	3½ starch 2½ lean meat
27	19	7	104	659	1 starch, 3 med. fat meat, 1 fat
12	13	5	48	374	½ starch, 1½ med. fat meat, 1 fat
20	26	9	128	489	1 starch, 2½ med. fat meat, 2 fat
12	8	3	80	207	½ starch, 1½ med. fat meat
19	9	2	35	680	1 starch, 2 med. fat meat
28	14	3	55	1020	1 starch, 3 med. fat meat

� = More than 800 milligrams sodium   ♥ = High amounts of sugar

Products	SERVING SIZE	CALORIES	CARBO-HYDRATE (gm)
Side Orders			
Garden Salad without Dressing	1 (7.8 oz.)	184	3
Side Salad without Dressing	1 (4 oz.)	20	1
⚓ Chef Salad without Dressing	1 (9.5 oz.)	214	5
🗄 Cole Slaw	4 oz.	240	13
🗄 ⚓ Cole Slaw	12 oz.	710	38
French Fries	Regular (2.5 oz.)	230	30
🗄 French Fries	Large (4 oz.)	360	48
🗄 Big Fry	1 (5.5 oz.)	500	66
🗄 ⚓ Crispy Curls	1 (3 oz.)	300	36
Mashed Potatoes	1 (4 oz.)	70	16
Mashed Potatoes	1 (12 oz.)	220	48
Gravy	1 (1.5 oz.)	20	3
Gravy	1 (5 oz.)	60	11

🗄 = More than 2 fat exchanges per serving

PROTEIN (gm)	FAT (gm)	SAT. FAT (gm)	CHOLES-TEROL (mg)	SODIUM (mg)	Exchanges
12	12	7	34	250	1 vegetable, 1½ med. fat meat, 1 fat
2	tr	tr	0	15	Free
20	13	8	44	910	1 vegetable, 2½ med. fat meat
2	20	3	10	340	2 vegetables, 4 fat
5	60	10	35	1020	2 vegetables, 1½ starch, 12 fat
3	11	2	0	85	2 starch, 2 fat
4	17	3	0	135	3 starch, 3 fat
6	23	5	0	180	4 starch, 4 fat
4	16	3	0	840	2 starch, 3 fat
2	tr	tr	0	260	1 starch
6	tr	tr	0	760	3 starch
1	tr	tr	0	260	Free
3	1	tr	5	850	1 starch

☀ = More than 800 milligrams sodium   ✿ = High amounts of sugar

Products	SERVING SIZE	CALORIES	CARBO-HYDRATE (gm)
Breakfast Items			
⒝ Rise N Shine Biscuit	1 (3 oz.)	320	34
⒝ Cinnamon 'N Raisin Biscuit	1 (3 oz.)	320	37
⒝ ⒯ Sausage Biscuit	1 (4 oz.)	440	34
⒝ ⒯ Sausage & Egg Biscuit	1 (5.3 oz.)	490	35
⒝ ⒯ Bacon Biscuit	1 (3.2 oz.)	360	34
⒝ ⒯ Bacon & Egg Biscuit	1 (4.4 oz.)	410	35
⒝ ⒯ Bacon, Egg, Cheese Biscuit	1 (4.8 oz.)	460	35
⒝ ⒯ Steak Biscuit	1 (5 oz.)	500	46
⒝ ⒯ Steak, Egg Biscuit	1 (6.3 oz.)	550	47
⒯ Chicken Biscuit	1 (5 oz.)	430	42
⒯ Ham Biscuit	1 (3.7 oz.)	320	34
⒯ Ham, Egg Biscuit	1 (4.9 oz.)	370	35

⒝ = More than 2 fat exchanges per serving

PROTEIN (gm)	FAT (gm)	SAT. FAT (gm)	CHOLES-TEROL (mg)	SODIUM (mg)	Exchanges
5	18	3	0	740	2 starch, 4 fat
4	17	5	0	510	2½ starch 3 fat
13	28	7	25	1100	2 starch, 1 high fat meat, 4 fat
18	31	8	170	1150	2 starch, 2 med. fat meat, 4 fat
10	21	4	10	950	2 starch, 4 fat
15	24	5	155	990	2 starch, 1 med. fat meat, 4 fat
17	28	8	165	1220	2 starch, 2 med. fat meat, 4 fat
15	29	7	30	1320	3 starch, 1 med. fat meat, 4 fat
20	32	8	175	1370	3 starch, 2 med. fat meat, 4 fat
17	22	4	45	1330	3 starch, 2 med. fat meat, 1 fat
10	16	2	15	1000	2 starch, 1 med. fat meat, 2 fat
15	19	4	160	1050	2 starch, 1½ med. fat meat, 2 fat

Ⓨ = More than 800 milligrams sodium   ❦ = High amounts of sugar

Products	SERVING SIZE	CALORIES	CARBO-HYDRATE (gm)
▊ ☀ Ham, Egg, Cheese Biscuit	1 (5.3 oz.)	420	35
▊ ☀ Country Ham Biscuit	1 (3.8 oz.)	350	35
▊ ☀ Country Ham, Egg Biscuit	1 (4.9 oz.)	400	35
▊ ☀ Canadian Rise N Shine Biscuit	1 (5.7 oz.)	470	35
▊ ☀ Big Country Breakfast Bacon	1 (7.6 oz.)	660	51
▊ ☀ Big Country Breakfast Ham	1 (8.8 oz.)	620	51
▊ ☀ Big Country Breakfast Sausage	1 (10 oz.)	850	51
▊ ☀ Big Country Breakfast Country Ham	1 (9 oz.)	670	52
▊ ☀ Ultimate Omelet Biscuit	1 (5.3 oz.)	540	36
▊ ☀ Frisco Sausage Breakfast Sandwich	1 (8 oz.)	720	43
☀ Frisco Ham Breakfast Sandwich	1 (6.5 oz.)	460	46

▊ = More than 2 fat exchanges per serving

PROTEIN (gm)	FAT (gm)	SAT. FAT (gm)	CHOLES- TEROL (mg)	SODIUM (mg)	Exchanges
18	23	6	170	1270	2 starch, 2 med. fat meat, 3 fat
11	18	3	25	1550	2 starch, 1 med. fat meat, 3 fat
16	22	4	175	1600	2 starch, 1½ med. fat meat, 3 fat
22	27	8	180	1550	2 starch, 2 med. fat meat, 4 fat
24	40	10	305	1540	3½ starch, 2 med. fat meat, 5 fat
28	33	7	325	1780	3½ starch, 2½ med. fat meat, 4 fat
33	57	16	340	1980	3½ starch, 3 med. fat meat, 8 fat
29	38	9	345	2870	3½ starch, 2½ med. fat meat, 5 fat
16	36	12	80	1120	2½ starch, 1 med. fat meat, 6 fat
33	47	17	205	1740	3 starch, 3 med. fat meat, 6 fat
20	22	8	175	1320	3 starch, 2 med. fat meat, 2 fat

� = More than 800 milligrams sodium   ♥ = High amounts of sugar

	Products	SERVING SIZE	CALORIES	CARBO-HYDRATE (gm)
🄱	Strawberry Cream Cheese Strudel	1 (3.5 oz.)	320	34
🄱	Hash Rounds Potatoes	1 (2.8 oz.)	230	24
🄱 🕇	Biscuit 'N Gravy	1 (8 oz.)	440	45
🕇	Pancakes	3 (4.8 oz.)	280	56
🕇	Pancakes with Sausage Pattie	3 (4.8 oz.) 1 (1.4 oz.)	430	56
🕇	Pancakes with Bacon Strips	3 (4.8 oz.) 2 (.5 oz.)	350	56
🄱	Blueberry Muffin	1 (4 oz.)	400	56
	Oatbran Raisin Muffin	1 (4.3 oz.)	410	59
	Orange Juice	11 oz.	140	34
	OCCASIONAL USE			
♥	Apple Turnover	1 (3.2 oz.)	270	38
♥	Big Cookie	1 1.7 oz.)	250	31
♥	Cool Twist Cone Chocolate	1 (4 oz.)	180	29
♥	Cool Twist Cone Vanilla	1 (4 oz.)	180	29

🄱 = More than 2 fat exchanges per serving

PROTEIN (gm)	FAT (gm)	SAT. FAT (gm)	CHOLES-TEROL (mg)	SODIUM (mg)	Exchanges
5	19	5	5	260	1 starch, 1 fruit 4 fat
3	14	3	0	560	1½ starch, 3 fat
9	24	6	15	1250	3 starch, 5 fat
8	2	1	15	890	3½ starch
16	16	6	40	1290	3½ starch 1 med. fat meat, 2 fat
13	9	3	25	1110	3½ starch 2 fat
7	17	4	65	310	3½ starch, 3 fat
8	16	3	50	380	4 starch 2 fat
2	tr	tr	0	5	2 fruit
3	12	4	0	250	2½ starch, 2 fat
3	13	4	5	240	2 starch, 2 fat
4	4	3	15	85	2 starch, 1 fat
5	4	3	15	80	2 starch, 1 fat

◢ = More than 800 milligrams sodium   ♥ = High amounts of sugar

Products	SERVING SIZE	CALORIES	CARBO-HYDRATE (gm)
☕ Cool Twist Cone Vanilla/Chocolate	1 (4 oz.)	170	29
☕ Vanilla Shake	1 (11.5 oz.)	370	59
☕ Chocolate Shake	1 (11.5 oz.)	390	61
☕ Strawberry Shake	1 (12 oz.)	390	65
☕ Butterfinger Shake	1 (12 oz.)	370	55
☕ Cool Twist Sundae Hot Fudge	1 (6 oz.)	320	50
☕ Cool Twist Sundae Caramel	1 (6 oz.)	330	59
☕ Cool Twist Sundae Strawberry	1 (6 oz.)	260	48

JACK IN THE BOX

Sandwiches

Hamburger	1 (3.4 oz.)	267	28
Cheeseburger	1 (4 oz.)	315	33
🅱 Double Cheeseburger	1 (5.25 oz.)	467	33
🅱 Jumbo Jack	1 (7.8 oz.)	584	42

🅱 = More than 2 fat exchanges per serving

PROTEIN (gm)	FAT (gm)	SAT. FAT (gm)	CHOLES- TEROL (mg)	SODIUM (mg)	Exchanges
5	4	3	15	85	2 starch, 1 fat
14	9	6	25	210	4 starch, 2 fat
15	10	6	31	220	4 starch, 2 fat
13	8	5	30	200	4 starch, 2 fat
12	9	6	32	180	4 starch, 2 fat
8	10	5	25	260	3 starch, 2 fat
6	8	4	20	280	4 starch, 2 fat
6	6	3	14	100	3 starch, 1 fat
13	11	4	26	556	2 starch, 1 med. fat meat, 1 fat
15	14	6	41	746	2 starch, 1 med. fat meat, 2 fat
21	27	12	72	842	2 starch, 2 med, fat meat, 3½ fat
26	34	11	73	733	3 starch, 2½ med. fat meat, 4 fat

☂ = More than 800 milligrams sodium   ♥ = High amounts of sugar

	Products	SERVING SIZE	CALORIES	CARBO-HYDRATE (gm)
🉐🕇	Jumbo Jack w/Cheese	1 (8.5 oz.)	667	46
🉐🕇	Old Fashioned Patty Melt	1 (7.5 oz.)	713	42
🉐🕇	Bacon Cheeseburger	1 (8.5 oz.)	705	41
🉐🕇	Grilled Sourdough Burger	1 (8 oz.)	712	34
🉐🕇	Ultimate Cheeseburger	1 (10 oz.)	942	33
	Chicken Fajita Pita	1 (6.6 oz.)	292	29
🕇	Chicken & Mushroom Sandwich	1 (7.8 oz.)	438	40
🉐🕇	Chicken Supreme	1 (8.6 oz.)	641	47
🉐🕇	Country Fried Steak Sandwich	1 (5.4 oz.)	450	42
🉐🕇	Fish Supreme	1 (7.7 oz.)	510	44
🕇	Grilled Chicken Fillet	1 (7.5 oz.)	431	36
🕇	Sirloin Steak Sandwich	1 (8.4 oz.)	517	49

🉐 = More than 2 fat exchanges per serving

PROTEIN (gm)	FAT (gm)	SAT. FAT (gm)	CHOLES- TEROL (mg)	SODIUM (mg)	Exchanges
32	40	14	102	1090	3 starch, 3½ med. fat meat, 4 fat
33	46	15	92	1360	3 starch, 3½ med. fat meat, 5 fat
35	45	15	113	1240	3 starch, 3½ med. fat meat, 5 fat
32	50	16	109	1140	2 starch, 4 med. fat meat, 6 fat
47	69	26	127	1176	2 starch, 6 med. fat meat, 8 fat
24	8	3	34	703	2 starch, 2½ lean meat
28	18	5	61	1340	2½ starch, 3 med. fat meat
27	39	10	85	1470	3 starch, 2½ med. fat meat, 5 fat
14	25	7	36	891	3 starch, 1 med. 3 fat
24	27	6	55	1040	3 starch, 2 med. fat meat, 3 fat
29	19	5	65	1070	2½ starch, 3 med. fat meat
29	23	5	66	1050	3 starch, 3 med. fat meat, 1 fat

☀ = More than 800 milligrams sodium   ♥ = High amounts of sugar

Products	SERVING SIZE	CALORIES	CARBO-HYDRATE (gm)
Side Orders			
🔋🕇 Seasoned Curly Fries	1 (3.8 oz.)	358	39
French Fries	Small (2.4 oz.)	219	28
🔋 French Fries	Regular (3.8 oz.)	351	45
🔋 French Fries	Jumbo (4.8 oz.)	396	51
🔋 Onion Rings	1 (3.6 oz.)	380	38
Sesame Breadsticks	1 (.5 oz.)	70	12
Tortilla Chips	1 (1 oz.)	139	18
Salads/Salad Dressings			
🕇 Chef Salad	1 (11.7 oz.)	325	10
🕇 Taco Salad	1 (14 oz.)	503	28
Side Salad	1 (4 oz.)	51	tr
🔋 Buttermilk House	2.5 oz.	362	8
🔋🕇 Bleu Cheese	2.5 oz.	262	14
🔋 Thousand Island	2.5 oz.	312	12

🔋 = More than 2 fat exchanges per serving

PROTEIN (gm)	FAT (gm)	SAT. FAT (gm)	CHOLES- TEROL (mg)	SODIUM (mg)	Exchanges
5	20	5	0	1030	2½ starch, 4 fat
3	11	3	0	121	2 starch, 2 fat
4	17	4	0	194	3 starch, 3 fat
5	19	5	0	219	3½ starch, 3 fat
5	23	6	0	451	2½ starch, 4 fat
2	2	tr	tr	110	1 starch
2	6	tr	tr	134	1 starch, 1 fat
30	18	8	142	900	2 vegetable, 4 med. fat meat
34	31	13	92	1600	2 starch, 4 med. fat meat, 1 fat
7	3	2	tr	84	1 lean meat
tr	36	6	21	694	½ starch, 7 fat
tr	22	4	18	918	1 starch, 4 fat
tr	30	5	23	700	1 starch, 5 fat

� = More than 800 milligrams sodium   ♣ = High amounts of sugar

Products	SERVING SIZE	CALORIES	CARBO-HYDRATE (gm)
✝ Low Calorie Italian	2.5 oz.	25	2
Mexican Food Taco	1 (2.75 oz.)	187	15
Super Taco	1 (4.5 oz.)	281	22
Guacamole	1 pkg. (1 oz.)	30	2
Salsa	1 pkg. (1 oz.)	8	2

Finger Foods

Products	SERVING SIZE	CALORIES	CARBO-HYDRATE (gm)
🔢✝ Egg Rolls	3 piece (5.8 oz.)	437	54
🔢✝ Egg Rolls	5 piece (10 oz.)	753	92
Chicken Strips	4 piece (4 oz.)	285	18
✝ Chicken Strips	6 piece (6.25 oz.)	451	28
🔢✝ Chicken Wings	6 piece (7.25 oz.)	846	78
🔢✝ Chicken Wings	9 piece (11 oz.)	1270	117

🔢 = More than 2 fat exchanges per serving

PROTEIN (gm)	FAT (gm)	SAT. FAT (gm)	CHOLES- TEROL (mg)	SODIUM (mg)	Exchanges
tr	2	tr	0	810	Free
7	11	4	18	414	1 starch, 1 med. fat meat, 1 fat
12	17	6	29	718	1½ starch, 1 med. fat meat, 2 fat
1	3	tr	0	128	½ fat
tr	tr	0	0	27	Free
3	24	7	29	957	3½ starch, 4 fat
5	41	12	49	1640	6 starch, 6 fat
25	13	3	52	695	1 starch, 3 med. fat meat
39	20	5	82	1100	2 starch, 4 med. fat meat
34	44	11	181	1710	5 starch, 3 med. fat meat, 5 fat
51	66	16	272	2560	7 starch, 4 med. fat meat, 9 fat

� = More than 800 milligrams sodium   ✿ = High amounts of sugar

	Products	SERVING SIZE	CALORIES	CARBO-HYDRATE (gm)
🅱	Mini Chimichangas	4 piece (7.3 oz.)	571	57
🅱 🕴	Mini Chimichangas	6 piece (11 oz.)	856	85
🅱	Toasted Raviolis	7 piece (5.75 oz.)	537	57
🅱 🕴	Toasted Raviolis	10 piece	768	81
	Sweet & Sour Sauce	1 oz.	40	11
	BBQ Sauce	1 oz.	44	11
	Hot Sauce	.5 oz.	4	1
	Italian Sauce	1.5 oz.	40	11

Breakfast Items

	Products	SERVING SIZE	CALORIES	CARBO-HYDRATE (gm)
	Orange Juice	6.5 oz.	80	20
🅱 🕴	Supreme Crescent	1 (5 oz.)	547	27
🅱 🕴	Sausage Crescent	1 (5.5 oz.)	584	28
🕴	Breakfast Jack	1 (4.5 oz.)	307	30
🅱 🕴	Pancake Platter	1 (8 oz.)	612	87

🅱 = More than 2 fat exchanges per serving

PROTEIN (gm)	FAT (gm)	SAT. FAT (gm)	CHOLES- TEROL (mg)	SODIUM (mg)	Exchanges
22	28	9	64	633	3½ starch, 2 med. fat meat, 3 fat
34	42	13	95	949	5 starch, 3 med. fat meat, 5 fat
15	28	8	36	639	4 starch, 5 fat
22	40	11	52	913	5 starch, 8 fat
tr	tr	0	tr	160	1 fruit
1	tr	tr	0	300	½ starch
tr	0	0	0	112	Free
tr	tr	tr	tr	176	½ starch
1	0	0	0	0	1 fruit
20	40	13	178	1053	2 starch, 2 med. fat meat, 6 fat
22	43	16	187	1012	2 starch, 2 med. fat meat, 6 fat
18	13	5	203	871	2 starch, 2 med. fat meat
15	22	9	99	888	5½ starch, 4 fat

☥ = More than 800 milligrams sodium   ♣ = High amounts of sugar

Products	SERVING SIZE	CALORIES	CARBO-HYDRATE (gm)
▤ ☥ Scrambled Egg Platter	1 (7.5 oz.)	559	50
☥ Scrambled Egg Pocket	1 (6.5 oz.)	431	31
☥ Sourdough Breakfast Sandwich	1 (5 oz.)	381	31
Hash Browns	1 (2 oz.)	156	14

OCCASIONAL USE

♥ Pancake Syrup	(1.5 oz.)	121	30
♥ ▤ Hot Apple Turnover	1 (4 oz.)	354	48
♥ ▤ Cheesecake	1 (3.5 oz.)	309	29
♥ Double Fudge Cake	1 (3 oz.)	288	49
♥ Vanilla Milk Shake	1 (11 oz.)	320	57
♥ Chocolate Milk Shake	1 (11.4 oz.)	330	55
♥ Strawberry Milk Shake	1 (11.6 oz.)	320	55

▤ = More than 2 fat exchanges per serving

PROTEIN (gm)	FAT (gm)	SAT. FAT (gm)	CHOLES- TEROL (mg)	SODIUM (mg)	Exchanges
18	32	9	378	1060	3 starch, 2 med. fat meat, 4 fat
29	21	8	354	1060	2 starch, 3 med. fat meat, 1 fat
21	20	7	236	1120	2 starch, 2 med. fat meat, 2 fat
1	11	3	0	312	1 starch, 2 fat
0	0	0	0	6	2 fruit
3	19	5	0	479	2 starch, 1 fruit 3 fat
8	18	9	63	208	2 starch, 3 fat
4	9	2	20	259	3 starch, 1 fat
10	6	4	25	230	4 starch
11	7	4	25	270	4 starch
10	7	4	25	240	4 starch

� = More than 800 milligrams sodium   ♥ = High amounts of sugar

Products	SERVING SIZE	CALORIES	CARBO-HYDRATE (gm)

KFC
Original Recipe Chicken

Products	SERVING SIZE	CALORIES	CARBO-HYDRATE (gm)
Wing	1 (1.9 oz.)	172	5
Side Breast	1 (2.9 oz.)	245	9
Center Breast	1 (3.6 oz.)	260	8
Drumstick	1 (2 oz.)	162	3
Thigh	1 (3.4 oz.)	287	8

Extra Crispy Chicken

Products	SERVING SIZE	CALORIES	CARBO-HYDRATE (gm)
Wing	1 (2 oz.)	231	8
🁢 Side Breast	1 (3.7 oz.)	379	16
Center Breast	1 (3.9 oz.)	344	15
Drumstick	1 (2.4 oz.)	205	7
🁢 Thigh	1 (4.2 oz.)	414	14

🁢 = More than 2 fat exchanges per serving

PROTEIN (gm)	FAT (gm)	SAT. FAT (gm)	CHOLES-TEROL (mg)	SODIUM (mg)	Exchanges
12	11	3	59	383	½ starch, 1½ med. fat meat, ½ fat
18	15	4	78	604	½ starch, 2½ med. fat meat, ½ fat
25	14	4	92	609	½ starch, 3 med. fat meat
14	9	2	75	269	2 med. fat meat
18	21	5	112	591	½ starch, 2 med. fat meat, 2 fat
11	17	4	63	319	½ starch, 1½ med. fat meat, 2 fat
19	27	7	77	646	1 starch, 2 med. fat meat, 3½ fat
23	21	5	80	636	1 starch, 3 med. fat meat, 1 fat
14	14	3	72	292	½ starch, 2 med. fat meat, ½ fat
20	31	8	112	580	1 starch, 2 med. fat meat, 4 fat

☝ = More than 800 milligrams sodium   ♥ = High amounts of sugar

Products	SERVING SIZE	CALORIES	CARBO-HYDRATE (gm)
Hot & Spicy Chicken			
Wing	1 (2.2 oz.)	244	9
⊟ 🕇 Side Breast	1 (4.1 oz.)	398	18
🕇 Center Breast	1 (4.3 oz.)	382	16
Drumstick	1 (2.5 oz.)	207	10
⊟ Thigh	1 (4.2 oz.)	412	16
KFC Skinfree Crispy Chicken			
Center Breast	1 (4 oz.)	296	11
Drumstick	1 (2 oz.)	166	8
Side Breast	1 (3.6 oz.)	293	11
Thigh	1 (3 oz.)	256	9
Kentucky Nuggets and Sauces			
🕇 Kentucky Nuggets	6 (3.4 oz.)	284	15

⊟ = More than 2 fat exchanges per serving

PROTEIN (gm)	FAT (gm)	SAT. FAT (gm)	CHOLES- TEROL (mg)	SODIUM (mg)	Exchanges
12	18	4	65	459	½ starch, 1½ med. fat meat, 2 fat
21	27	7	83	922	1 starch, 2½ med. fat meat, 3 fat
24	25	6	84	905	1 starch, 3 med. fat meat, 2 fat
11	14	3	75	406	1 starch, 1 med. fat meat, 1 fat
19	30	8	105	750	1 starch, 2 med. fat meat. 4 fat
24	16	3	59	435	1 starch, 3 med. fat meat
13	9	2	42	256	½ starch, 2 med. fat meat
22	17	4	83	410	1 starch, 3 med. fat meat
17	17	4	68	394	½ starch, 2 med. fat meat, 1 fat
16	18	4	66	865	1 starch, 2 med. fat meat, 1 fat

☀ = More than 800 milligrams sodium   ❦ = High amounts of sugar

Products	SERVING SIZE	CALORIES	CARBO-HYDRATE (gm)
Barbeque Sauce	1 oz.	35	7
Sweet & Sour Sauce	1 oz.	58	13
Mustard Sauce	1 oz.	36	6

Side Orders

Products	SERVING SIZE	CALORIES	CARBO-HYDRATE (gm)
Chicken Littles Sandwich	1 (1.7 oz.)	169	14
▌🌴 Colonel's Chicken Sandwich	1 (5.9 oz.)	482	39
▌🌴 Hot Wings	6 (4.8 oz.)	471	18
Buttermilk Biscuits	1 (2.3 oz.)	235	28
Mashed Potatoes w/Gravy	1 (3.5 oz.)	71	12
French Fries	1 (2.7 oz.)	244	31
▌ Crispy Fries	1 (3.1 oz.)	294	33
Potato Salad	1 (3 oz.)	141	13
Baked Beans	1 (3 oz.)	105	18
Corn-on-the-Cob	1 (2.6 oz.)	90	16
Cole Slaw	1 (3.2 oz.)	114	13

▌ = More than 2 fat exchanges per serving

PROTEIN (gm)	FAT (gm)	SAT. FAT (gm)	CHOLES-TEROL (mg)	SODIUM (mg)	Exchanges
tr	1	0	tr	450	½ starch or fruit
tr	1	0	tr	148	1 starch or fruit
1	1	0	tr	346	½ starch or fruit
6	10	2	18	331	1 starch, ½ med. fat meat, 1 fat
21	27	6	47	1060	2½ starch, 2 med. fat meat, 3 fat
27	33	8	150	1230	1 starch, 3 med. fat meat, 4 fat
5	12	3	1	655	2 starch, 2 fat
3	2	0	tr	339	1 starch
3	12	3	2	139	2 starch, 2 fat
4	17	4	3	761	2 starch, 3 fat
2	9	NA	NA	396	1 starch, 2 fat
5	1	NA	NA	387	1 starch
3	2	1	tr	11	1 starch
1	6	1	4	177	2 vegetable or 1 starch, 1 fat

� = More than 800 milligrams sodium   ♣ = High amounts of sugar

Products	SERVING SIZE	CALORIES	CARBO-HYDRATE (gm)

LONG JOHN SILVER'S

Meals

	Products	SERVING SIZE	CALORIES	CARBO-HYDRATE (gm)
目 ⛫	Fish & Fries, 2 hushpuppies, & slaw	2 pc. Fish (14.4 oz.)	890	92
目 ⛫	Fish & Fries 2 hushpuppies	2 pc. Fish (9.2 oz.)	610	52
目 ⛫	Chicken Planks w/fries & slaw 2 hushpuppies	3 pc. (14.1 oz.)	890	101
目 ⛫	Chicken Planks & Fries	2 pc. (6.9 oz.)	490	50
目 ⛫	Clam 6 oz. w/ fries & slaw, 2 hushpuppies	1 (12.7 oz.)	990	114
目 ⛫	Battered Shrimp w/ fries & slaw 2 hushpuppies	10 pc (11.7 oz.)	840	88
目 ⛫	Fish, Chicken & Fries	1 pc. Fish 1 pc. Chicken (8.1 oz.)	550	51
目 ⛫	Fish & Chicken w/ fries & slaw	1 pc. Fish 2 pc. Chicken (15.2 oz.)	950	102

目 = More than 2 fat exchanges per serving

PROTEIN (gm)	FAT (gm)	SAT. FAT (gm)	CHOLES-TEROL (mg)	SODIUM (mg)	Exchanges
31	48	10	75	1790	5 starch, 1 vegetable, 3 med. fat meat, 6 fat
27	37	8	60	1480	3½ starch, 3 med. fat meat, 3 fat
32	44	10	55	2000	6 starch, 2 vegetable, 3 med. fat meat, 4 fat
19	26	6	30	1290	3 starch, 2 med. fat meat, 3 fat
24	52	11	75	1830	7 starch, 1 vegetable, 2 med. fat meat, 6 fat
18	47	10	100	1630	5 starch, 1 vegetable 2 med. fat meat, 7 fat
23	32	7	45	1380	3 starch, 2 med. fat meat, 4 fat
36	49	11	75	2090	6 starch, 1 vegetable, 4 med. fat meat, 4 fat

☂ = More than 800 milligrams sodium   ♠ = High amounts of sugar

Products	SERVING SIZE	CALORIES	CARBO-HYDRATE (gm)
▯ ⸸ Fish & Shrimp w/ fries & slaw,	2 pc. Fish 8 Shrimp (17.2 oz.)	1140	108
▯ ⸸ Shrimp, Fish, Chicken w/ fries & slaw,	2 pc. Fish 5 Shrimp 1 pc. Chicken (18.1 oz.)	1160	113
▯ ⸸ Fish, Shrimp, & Clams w/fries & slaw	2 pc. Fish 4 Shrimp 3 oz. Clams (18.1 oz.)	1240	123
⸸ Baked Fish w/Lemon Crumb, Rice, Green Beans, Slaw, Roll	3 pc. Fish (17.4 oz.)	570	80
Light Portion Fish w/Lemon Crumb, Rice, Salad	2 pc. Fish (9.8 oz.)	270	37
⸸ Baked Chicken Rice, Green Beans, Slaw, Roll	1 meal (16 oz.)	550	76

Sandwiches

Products	SERVING SIZE	CALORIES	CARBO-HYDRATE (gm)
⸸ Batter-dipped Fish	1 pc. Fish (5.6 oz.)	340	40
Batter-dipped Chicken	1 pc. Chicken (4.5 oz.)	280	39

▯ = More than 2 fat exchanges per serving

PROTEIN (gm)	FAT (gm)	SAT. FAT (gm)	CHOLES- TEROL (mg)	SODIUM (mg)	Exchanges
40	65	14	145	2440	6 starch, 1 vegetable, 4 med. fat meat, 8 fat
45	65	14	135	2590	7 starch, 1 vegetable, 4½ med. fat meat, 6 fat
44	70	15	140	2630	7 starch, 2 vegetable, 4 med. fat meat, 8 fat
39	12	2	124	1470	4 starch, 2 vegetable, 4 lean meat,
23	5	1	75	680	2 starch, 1 vegetable, 2 lean meat
32	15	3	75	1670	4 starch, 2 vegetable 3 med. fat meat
18	13	3	30	890	2½ starch, 2 med. fat meat
14	8	2	15	790	2½ starch, 1 med. fat meat

☥ = More than 800 milligrams sodium   ♥ = High amounts of sugar

Products	SERVING SIZE	CALORIES	CARBO-HYDRATE (gm)
Kid's Meals			
Fish & Fries 1 hushpuppy	1 pc. Fish (7 oz.)	500	50
Chicken Planks & Fries	2 pc. (7.8 oz.)	560	60
Fish, Chicken & Fries	1 pc. Fish 1 Chicken (8.9 oz.)	620	61
Salads			
Seafood Salad without crackers	1 (9.8 oz.)	380	12
Ocean Chef Salad without crackers	1 (8.3 oz.)	110	13
Small Salad	1 (2.4 oz.)	14	3
Finger Foods			
Batter-Dipped Fish	1 pc. (3.1 oz.)	180	12
Chicken Planks	2 pc. (4 oz.)	240	22
A La Carte			
Battered Fish	1 pc. (3.1 oz.)	180	12

▌ = More than 2 fat exchanges per serving

PROTEIN (gm)	FAT (gm)	SAT. FAT (gm)	CHOLES-TEROL (mg)	SODIUM (mg)	Exchanges
16	28	6	30	1010	3 starch, 1 med. fat meat, 4 fat
21	29	6	30	1310	4 starch, 2 med. fat meat, 2 fat
24	34	7	45	1400	4 starch, 2 med. fat meat, 4 fat
15	31	5	55	980	2 vegetable, 2 med. fat meat, 4 fat
12	1	tr	40	730	2 vegetable, 2 lean meat
tr	tr	tr	0	10	1 vegetable
12	11	3	30	490	1 starch, 1 med. fat meat, 1 fat
16	12	3	30	790	1½ starch, 2 med. fat meat
12	11	3	30	490	1 starch, 1 med. fat meat, 1 fat

� = More than 800 milligrams sodium   ♥ = High amounts of sugar

Products	SERVING SIZE	CALORIES	CARBO-HYDRATE (gm)
Chicken Plank	1 pc. (2 oz.)	120	11
Breaded Shrimp	1 pc. (.4 oz.)	30	2
Baked Fish w/Lemon Crumb	3 pc. (5 oz.)	150	4
Chicken Light Herb	1 pc. (3.5 oz.)	120	tr
Seafood Gumbo w/Cod	1 order (7 oz.)	120	4
Seafood Chowder w/Cod	1 order (7 oz.)	140	10
Fries	1 order (3 oz.)	220	28
Hushpuppies	1 pc.	70	10
Cole Slaw	1 order	140	20
Corn Cobbette	1 pc. (3.3 oz.)	140	18
Green Beans	1 order (3.5 oz.)	20	3
Rice	1 order (4 oz.)	160	30
Roll	1 (1.5 oz.)	110	23

B = More than 2 fat exchanges per serving

PROTEIN (gm)	FAT (gm)	SAT. FAT (gm)	CHOLES-TEROL (mg)	SODIUM (mg)	Exchanges
8	6	2	15	400	1 starch, 1 med. fat meat
1	2	tr	10	80	Free
29	1	tr	110	370	3 lean meat
22	4	1	60	570	3 lean meat
9	8	2	25	740	1 vegetable, 1 med. fat meat
11	6	2	20	590	1 starch, 1 med. fat meat
3	15	3	0	500	2 starch, 2 fat
2	2	tr	5	25	½ starch, ½ fat
1	6	1	15	260	1 starch, 1 fat
3	8	1	0	0	1 starch, 1½ fat
1	tr	tr	0	320	1 vegetable
3	3	tr	0	340	2 starch
4	tr	tr	0	170	1½ starch

*= More than 800 milligrams sodium ♥ = High amounts of sugar

Products	SERVING SIZE	CALORIES	CARBO-HYDRATE (gm)
Condiments			
Seafood Sauce	½ oz.	14	3
Tartar Sauce	½ oz.	50	2
☖ Ranch Dressing	1 oz.	180	tr
Creamy Italian Dressing	1 oz.	30	tr
☖ Sea Salad Dressing	1 oz.	140	2
OCCASIONAL USE			
☙ Apple Pie	4.5 oz.	320	43
☙ Cherry Pie	4.5 oz.	360	55
☙ Lemon Pie	4 oz.	340	60
☖ ☙ Walnut Brownie	3.4 oz.	440	54
☙ Oatmeal Raisin Cookie	1.8 oz.	160	15
☙ Chocolate Chip Cookie	1.8 oz.	230	35

☖ = More than 2 fat exchanges per serving

PROTEIN (gm)	FAT (gm)	SAT. FAT (gm)	CHOLES- TEROL (mg)	SODIUM (mg)	Exchanges
tr	tr	0	0	180	Free
tr	5	1	0	35	1 fat
tr	19	4	5	230	4 fat
tr	3	tr	tr	280	1 fat
tr	15	6	5	160	3 fat
3	13	5	5	420	3 starch, 2 fat
4	13	4	5	200	3½ starch, 2 fat
7	9	3	45	130	4 starch, 1 fat
5	22	5	20	150	3½ starch, 4 fat
3	10	2	15	150	1 starch, 2 fat
3	9	6	10	170	2 starch, 2 fat

🍗 = More than 800 milligrams sodium   🍬 = High amounts of sugar

Products	SERVING SIZE	CALORIES	CARBO-HYDRATE (gm)
MCDONALD'S			
Sandwiches			
Hamburger	1 (3.6 oz.)	255	30
Cheeseburger	1 (4 oz.)	305	30
Quarter Pounder	1 (5.9 oz.)	410	34
ⵌ Quarter Pounder w/Cheese	1 (6.8 oz.)	510	34
ⵌ Big Mac	1 (7.6 oz.)	500	42
Filet-O-Fish	1 (5 oz.)	370	38
McLean Deluxe	1 (7.3 oz.)	320	35
ⵌ McLean Deluxe with Cheese	1 (7.7 oz.)	370	35
ⵌ McChicken	1 ((6.5 oz.)	415	39
Chicken Fajitas	1 (2.9 oz.)	190	20

ⵌ = More than 2 fat exchanges per serving

PROTEIN (gm)	FAT (gm)	SAT. FAT (gm)	CHOLES- TEROL (mg)	SODIUM (mg)	Exchanges
12	9	3	37	490	2 starch, 1 med. fat meat, 1 fat
15	13	5	50	725	2 starch, 1½ med. fat meat, 1 fat
23	20	8	85	645	2 starch, 3 med. fat meat, 1 fat
28	28	11	115	1110	2 starch, 3½ med. fat meat, 2 fat
25	26	9	100	890	3 starch, 2½ med. fat meat, 2 fat
14	18	4	50	730	2½ starch, 1 med. fat meat, 2 fat
22	10	4	60	670	2 starch, 3 lean meat
24	14	5	75	890	2 starch, 3 lean meat, 1 fat
19	20	4	50	830	2½ starch, 2 med. fat meat, 2 fat
11	8	2	35	310	1 starch, 1 lean meat, 1 fat

🍴 = More than 800 milligrams sodium   🍬 = High amounts of sugar

Products	SERVING SIZE	CALORIES	CARBO-HYDRATE (gm)
Chicken McNuggets/Sauces			
Chicken McNuggets	4 piece (2.6 oz.)	180	11
Chicken McNuggets	6 piece (3.9 oz.)	270	17
Chicken McNuggets	9 piece (5.9 oz.)	405	25
Hot Mustard Sauce	1 (1 oz.)	70	8
Barbeque Sauce	1 (1.1 oz.)	50	12
Sweet and Sour Sauce	1 (1.1 oz.)	60	14
12 " Family Size Pizza			
Cheese	1 slice (2.6 oz.)	178	24
Deluxe	1 slice (3.4 oz.)	216	24
Pepperoni	1 slice (2.8 oz.)	208	23
Sausage	1 slice (3 oz.)	216	23

🯰 = More than 2 fat exchanges per serving

PROTEIN (gm)	FAT (gm)	SAT. FAT (gm)	CHOLES-TEROL (mg)	SODIUM (mg)	Exchanges
13	10	2	35	390	1 starch, 1½ med. fat meat
20	15	4	55	580	1 starch, 2 med. fat meat, 1 fat
30	22	5	85	870	1½ starch, 3 med. fat meat, 1½ fat
0	4	tr	5	250	½ fruit, ½ fat
0	tr	0	0	340	1 fruit
0	tr	0	0	190	1 fruit
10	7	3	14	399	1½ starch, 1 med. fat meat
10	8	4	20	549	1½ starch, 1 med. fat meat
10	7	3	18	523	1½ starch, 1 med. fat meat
10	8	4	22	530	1½ starch, 1 med. fat meat

☀ = More than 800 milligrams sodium ♥ = High amounts of sugar

Products	SERVING SIZE	CALORIES	CARBO-HYDRATE (gm)
French Fries			
French Fries	Small (2.4 oz.)	220	26
⏟ French Fries	Medium (3.4 oz.)	320	36
⏟ French Fries	Large (4.3 oz.)	400	46
Salads			
Chef Salad	1 (9.3 oz.)	170	8
Garden Salad	1 (6.6 oz.)	50	6
Chunky Chicken Salad	1 (9 oz.)	150	7
Side Salad	1 (3.7 oz.)	30	4
Croutons	.4 oz.	50	7
Bacon Bits	.1 oz.	15	0
Salad Dressings			
⏟ Blue Cheese	.5 oz. / 2.5 oz. packet	50 / 225	1 / 5
⏟ Ranch	.5 oz. / 2 oz. packet	55 / 220	1 / 4
⏟ 1000 Island	.5 oz. / 2.5 oz.	45 / 225	4 / 20

⏟ = More than 2 fat exchanges per serving

PROTEIN (gm)	FAT (gm)	SAT. FAT (gm)	CHOLES-TEROL (mg)	SODIUM (mg)	Exchanges
3	12	3	0	110	2 starch, 2 fat
4	17	4	0	150	2½ starch, 3 fat
6	22	5	0	200	3 starch, 4 fat
17	9	4	111	400	1 vegetable, 2 med. fat meat
4	2	tr	65	70	1 vegetable
25	4	1	78	230	1 vegetable, 3 lean meat
2	1	tr	33	85	1 vegetable
1	2	1	0	140	½ starch
1	1	tr	1	95	Free
0	4	1	7	150	1 fat
0	20	5	35	750	5 fat
0	5	1	5	130	1 fat
0	25	5	25	650	5 fat
0	3	1	8	100	1 fat
0	15	5	40	500	5 fat

☀ = More than 800 milligrams sodium   ♣ = High amounts of sugar

Products	SERVING SIZE	CALORIES	CARBO-HYDRATE (gm)
Lite Vinaigrette	.5 oz.	12	2
	2 oz. packet	48	8
Red French Reduced Calorie	.5 oz.	40	5
	2 oz. packet	160	20

Breakfast

Products	SERVING SIZE	CALORIES	CARBO-HYDRATE (gm)
Egg McMuffin	1 (4.8 oz.)	280	28
Sausage McMuffin	1 (4.8 oz.)	345	27
ⵙ Sausage McMuffin w/Egg	1 (5.6 oz.)	430	27
Scrambled Eggs	2 (3.5 oz.)	140	1
Sausage	1 (1.5 oz.)	160	0
English Muffin with Spread	1 (2 oz.)	170	26
Hash Brown Potatoes	1 (1.9 oz.)	130	15
Biscuit with Biscuit Spread	1 (2.6 oz.)	260	32
日 ⵙ Sausage Biscuit	1 (4.2 oz.)	420	32

日 = More than 2 fat exchanges per serving

PROTEIN (gm)	FAT (gm)	SAT. FAT (gm)	CHOLES- TEROL (mg)	SODIUM (mg)	Exchanges
0	1	tr	0	60	Free
0	4	1	0	240	1 fat
0	2	tr	0	115	1 fat
0	9	1	0	460	1 starch, 2 fat
18	11	4	235	710	2 starch, 2 med. fat meat
15	20	7	57	770	2 starch, 1½ med. fat meat, 2 fat
21	25	3	270	920	2 starch, 2½ med. fat meat, 2 fat
12	10	3	425	290	2 med. fat meat
7	15	5	43	310	1 med. fat meat, 2 fat
5	4	1	0	285	2 starch, 1 fat
1	7	2	1	330	1 starch, 1 fat
5	13	3	1	730	2 starch, 2 fat
12	28	8	44	1040	2 starch, 1 med. fat meat, 4 fat

☎ = More than 800 milligrams sodium   ♥ = High amounts of sugar

Products	SERVING SIZE	CALORIES	CARBO-HYDRATE (gm)
𝔹 ⚕ Sausage Biscuit with Egg	1 (6.2 oz.)	505	33
𝔹 ⚕ Bacon, Egg and Cheese Biscuit	1 (5.4 oz.)	440	33
Breakfast Burrito	1 (3.7 oz.)	280	21
Cheerios	¾ cup	80	14
Wheaties	¾ cup	90	19
Fat-Free Apple Bran	1 (2.6 oz.)	180	40
Hot Cakes (plain) Margarine ⚚ Syrup	1 order 2 pats 1½ fl. oz.	250 70 120	44 0 30
Orange, Grapefruit or Apple Juice	6 oz.	80	19

OCCASIONAL USE

𝔹 ⚚ Baked Apple Pie	1 (3 oz.)	280	35
⚚ McDonaldland Cookies	1 box (2 oz.)	290	47
𝔹 ⚚ Chocolate Chip Cookies	1 box (2 oz.)	330	42
⚚ Vanilla Lowfat Frozen Yogurt Cone	1 (3 oz.)	105	22

𝔹 = More than 2 fat exchanges per serving

PROTEIN (gm)	FAT (gm)	SAT. FAT (gm)	CHOLES-TEROL (mg)	SODIUM (mg)	Exchanges
19	33	10	260	1210	2 starch, 2 med. meat, 4 fat
15	26	8	240	1215	2 starch, 2 med. fat meat, 3 fat
12	17	4	135	580	1½ starch, 1 med. fat meat, 2 fat
3	1	tr	0	210	1 starch
2	1	tr	0	220	1 starch
5	0	0	0	200	2½ starch
3	2	2	8	570	3 starch, ½ fat
0	8	2	0	110	1½ fat
0	0	0	0	5	2 fruit
1	0	0	0	0	1 fruit
3	15	2	0	90	1 starch, 1 fruit, 3 fat
4	7	1	0	300	3 starch, 1 fat
4	15	4	4	280	2½ starch, 3 fat
4	1	tr	3	80	1½ starch

☝ = More than 800 milligrams sodium   ♥ = High amounts of sugar

Products	SERVING SIZE	CALORIES	CARBO-HYDRATE (gm)
♥ Strawberry Lowfat Frozen Yogurt Sundae	1 (6 oz.)	210	49
♥ Hot Fudge Frozen Yogurt Sundae	1 (6 oz.)	240	50
♥ Hot Caramel Frozen Yogurt Sundae	1 (6 oz.)	270	59
♥ Vanilla Lowfat Milk Shake	1 (10.4 oz.)	290	60
♥ Chocolate Lowfat Milk Shake	1 (10.4 oz.)	320	66
♥ Strawberry Lowfat Milk Shake	1 (10.4 oz.)	320	67
🞌 ♥ Apple Danish	1 (4 oz.)	390	51
🞌 ♥ Iced Cheese Danish	1 (3.9 oz.)	390	42
🞌 ♥ Cinnamon Raisin Danish	1 (3.9 oz.)	440	58
🞌 ♥ Raspberry Danish	1 (4.1 oz.)	410	62

🞌 = More than 2 fat exchanges per serving

PROTEIN (gm)	FAT (gm)	SAT. FAT (gm)	CHOLES- TEROL (mg)	SODIUM (mg)	Exchanges
6	1	tr	5	95	2 starch, 1 fruit
7	3	2	6	170	2 starch, 1½ fruit
7	3	2	13	180	2 starch, 2 fruit
11	1	tr	10	170	4 starch
11	2	1	10	240	4 starch
11	1	tr	10	170	4 starch
6	17	4	25	370	3 starch, 3 fat
7	21	6	47	420	3 starch, 4 fat
6	21	5	34	430	4 starch, 3 fat
6	16	3	26	310	4 starch, 2 fat

☫ = More than 800 milligrams sodium   ♥ = High amounts of sugar

Products	SERVING SIZE	CALORIES	CARBO-HYDRATE (gm)
PIZZA HUT			
Thin 'N Crispy			
Cheese	1 slice of medium pizza	223	19
Beef	1 slice of medium pizza	231	20
Pepperoni	1 slice of medium pizza	230	20
Italian Sausage	1 slice of medium pizza	282	20
Pork	1 slice of medium pizza	240	20
☀ Meat Lovers	1 slice of medium pizza	297	20
Veggie Lovers	1 slice of medium pizza	192	20
☀ Pepperoni Lovers	1 slice of medium pizza	320	20
☀ Supreme	1 slice of medium pizza	262	20
Super Supreme	1 slice of medium pizza	253	20

☐ = More than 2 fat exchanges per serving

PROTEIN (gm)	FAT (gm)	SAT. FAT (gm)	CHOLES-TEROL (mg)	SODIUM (mg)	Exchanges
13	10	5	25	503	1 starch, 1½ med fat meat, 1 fat
13	11	3	25	705	1 starch, 1½ med fat meat, 1 fat
12	11	3	27	678	1 starch, 1½ med fat meat, 1 fat
14	17	6	38	781	1 starch, 1½ med fat meat, 2 fat
13	12	3	25	713	1 starch, 1½ med fat meat, 1 fat
14	16	4	44	1068	1 starch, 2 med fat meat, 2 fat
11	8	3	17	551	1 starch, 1½ med fat meat
18	19	4	46	949	1 starch, 2 med fat meat, 2 fat
15	14	3	31	819	1 starch, 2 med fat meat, 1 fat
16	12	3	35	700	1 starch, 2 med fat meat, ½ fat

☂ = More than 800 milligrams sodium   ♣ = High amounts of sugar

Products	SERVING SIZE	CALORIES	CARBO-HYDRATE (gm)
Hand Tossed			
Cheese	1 slice of medium pizza	253	27
Beef	1 slice of medium pizza	261	28
Pepperoni	1 slice of medium pizza	283	28
⍓ Italian Sausage	1 slice of medium pizza	313	27
⍓ Pork	1 slice of medium pizza	270	28
⍓ Meat Lovers	1 slice of medium pizza	321	28
Veggie Lovers	1 slice of medium pizza	222	28
⍓ Pepperoni Lovers	1 slice of medium pizza	335	28
⍓ Supreme	1 slice of medium pizza	289	28
⍓ Super Supreme	1 slice of medium pizza	276	28

⍓ = More than 2 fat exchanges per serving

PROTEIN (gm)	FAT (gm)	SAT. FAT (gm)	CHOLES- TEROL (mg)	SODIUM (mg)	Exchanges
15	9	4	25	593	2 starch, 1½ med fat meat
15	10	3	25	795	2 starch, 1½ med fat meat
20	10	3	25	738	2 starch, 2 med fat meat
16	15	6	38	871	2 starch, 1½ med fat meat, 1 fat
15	11	3	25	803	2 starch, 1½ med fat meat
16	15	4	42	1106	2 starch, 1½ med fat meat, 1 fat
13	7	3	17	641	2 starch, 1½ lean meat
19	16	4	43	981	2 starch, 2 med fat meat, 1 fat
17	12	3	29	894	2 starch, 1½ med fat meat, ½ fat
17	10	3	32	980	2 starch, 1½ med fat meat

♛ = More than 800 milligrams sodium   ♛ = High amounts of sugar

Products	SERVING SIZE	CALORIES	CARBO-HYDRATE (gm)
Pan			
Cheese	1 slice of medium pizza	279	26
Beef	1 slice of medium pizza	288	27
Pepperoni	1 slice of medium pizza	280	26
🐵 Italian Sausage	1 slice of medium pizza	399	26
Pork	1 slice of medium pizza	296	27
🕯 Meat Lovers	1 slice of medium pizza	347	27
Veggie Lovers	1 slice of medium pizza	249	27
🐵🕯 Pepperoni Lovers	1 slice of medium pizza	362	27
Supreme	1 slice of medium pizza	315	27
🕯 Super Supreme	1 slice of medium pizza	302	27
Bigfoot			
🕯 Cheese	1 slice	179	24

🐵 = More than 2 fat exchanges per serving

PROTEIN (gm)	FAT (gm)	SAT. FAT (gm)	CHOLES-TEROL (mg)	SODIUM (mg)	Exchanges
14	13	5	35	473	2 starch, 1½ med fat meat, 1 fat
10	18	3	25	675	2 starch, 1 med fat meat, 2 fat
8	18	3	25	618	2 starch, I med fat meat, 2 fat
15	24	6	38	751	2 starch, 1½ med fat meat, 3 fat
10	19	3	25	683	2 starch, 1 med fat meat, 2 fat
15	23	5	42	986	2 starch, 1½ med fat meat, 2 fat
7	15	3	17	521	2 starch, 2 fat
14	25	5	34	861	2 starch, 1½ med fat meat, 3 fat
16	16	3	29	774	2 starch, 1½ med fat meat, 1 fat
12	19	4	32	860	2 starch, 1 med fat meat, 2 fat
9	5	3	14	959	1½ starch, 1 med fat meat

✱ = More than 800 milligrams sodium ♥ = High amounts of sugar

Products	SERVING SIZE	CALORIES	CARBO-HYDRATE (gm)
�ᵀ Pepperoni	1 slice	195	24
ᵀ Pepperoni, Italian Sausage, Mushroom	1 slice	213	25
Personal Pan Pizza			
ᵀ Pepperoni	1 whole	675	76
ᵀ Supreme	1 whole	647	76

RAX

Sandwiches

Regular Rax	1 (4.7 oz.)	262	25
日 ᵀ Deluxe Roast Beef Sandwich	1 (7.9 oz.)	498	39
日 ᵀ Beef, Bacon 'n Cheddar	1 (6.7 oz.)	523	37
ᵀ Philly Melt	1 (8.2 oz.)	396	40
日 ᵀ Country Fried Chicken Breast Sandwich	1 (7.4 oz.)	618	49

日 = More than 2 fat exchanges per serving

PROTEIN (gm)	FAT (gm)	SAT. FAT (gm)	CHOLES- TEROL (mg)	SODIUM (mg)	Exchanges
10	7	3	17	1022	1½ starch, 1 med fat meat
10	8	4	21	1208	1½ starch, I med fat meat, ½ fat
36	29	NA	53	1335	5 starch, 3 med fat meat, 2 fat
37	28	NA	53	1313	5 starch, 3 med fat meat, 1 fat
18	10	4	15	707	1½ starch, 2 med. fat meat
21	30	7	36	864	2½ starch, 2 med. fat meat, 3 fat
24	32	8	42	1042	2½ starch, 2½ med. fat meat, 3 fat
25	16	7	27	1055	2½ starch, 2½ med. fat meat
23	29	15	45	1078	3 starch, 3 med. fat meat, 3 fat

🛉 = More than 800 milligrams sodium   🍬 = High amounts of sugar

Products	SERVING SIZE	CALORIES	CARBO-HYDRATE (gm)
✝ Grilled Chicken	1 (6.9 oz.)	402	26

Side Orders

French Fries	Regular (3.25 oz.)	282	36
Baked Potato	1 (10 oz.)	264	61
Baked Potato w/Margarine	1 (10.5 oz.) (1 tbsp.)	364	61

Salads

Gourmet Garden Salad without Dressing	1 salad (8.7 oz.)	134	13
⽇ with French Dressing	1 (10.7 oz.)	409	33
with Lite Italian Dressing	1 (10.7 oz.)	196	22
Grilled Chicken Garden Salad without Dressing	1 (10.7 oz.)	202	14
⽇ ✝ with French Dressing	1 (12.7 oz.)	477	34

⽇ = More than 2 fat exchanges per serving

PROTEIN (gm)	FAT (gm)	SAT. FAT (gm)	CHOLES-TEROL (mg)	SODIUM (mg)	Exchanges
25	23	4	69	872	2 starch, 3 med. fat meat, 1 fat
3	14	4	3	75	2½ starch, 2 fat
6	0	0	0	15	4 starch
6	11	2	0	115	4 starch, 2 fat
7	6	2	2	350	2 vegetable, 1 med. fat meat
7	29	5	2	792	2 vegetable, 1 fruit, 1 med. fat meat, 5 fat
7	10	2	2	643	2 vegetable, ½ fruit, 1 med. fat meat, 1 fat
19	9	2	32	747	2 vegetable, 2 med. fat meat
19	31	6	32	1189	2 vegetable, 1 fruit, 2 med. fat meat, 4 fat

☀ = More than 800 milligrams sodium   ♥ = High amounts of sugar

Products	SERVING SIZE	CALORIES	CARBO-HYDRATE (gm)
✶ with Lite Italian Dressing	(12.7 oz.)	264	22

Condiments

Mushroom Sauce	1 oz.	16	1
Swiss Slice	.4 oz.	42	0
Barbecue Sauce	1 packet	11	3
Cheddar Cheese Sauce	1 oz.	29	4
Bacon Slice	.1 oz.	14	0
ȸ French Dressing	2 oz.	275	20
Lite Italian Dressing	2 oz.	63	8

OCCASIONAL USE

☛ Chocolate Chip Cookies	2 cookies (2 oz,)	262	36
Colombo Yogurt Shakes			
☛ Vanilla Fat Free Shakes	10.25 oz.	220	44
☛ Chocolate Fat Free Shakes	11.25 oz.	310	66
☛ Strawberry Fat Free Shakes	11.25 oz.	300	64

ȸ = More than 2 fat exchanges per serving

PROTEIN (gm)	FAT (gm)	SAT. FAT (gm)	CHOLES- TEROL (mg)	SODIUM (mg)	Exchanges
19	12	3	32	1040	2 vegetable, ½ fruit, 2 med. fat meat
1	tr	0	0	113	Free
3	3	2	10	157	½ med. fat meat
0	0	0	0	158	Free
tr	tr	0	2	40	Free
1	1	tr	2	40	Free
0	22	3	0	442	1 fruit, 4 fat
0	3	0	0	294	½ fruit, ½ fat
4	12	4	6	192	2 starch, 2 fat
9	tr	NA	0	140	3 starch
10	tr	NA	0	180	4 starch
9	tr	NA	0	150	4 starch

☂ = More than 800 milligrams sodium   ♥ = High amounts of sugar

	Products	SERVING SIZE	CALORIES	CARBO-HYDRATE (gm)
♥	Candy Cane Regular Shake	12.10 oz.	320	62
♥	Cool Orange Regular Shake	12 oz.	360	65
♥	Peach Regular Shake	12 oz.	320	60
♥	Blackberry Regular Shake	11.25 oz.	270	58
♥	Mocha Regular Shake	11.75 oz.	350	64

NOT RECOMMENDED FOR USE

	Products	SERVING SIZE	CALORIES	CARBO-HYDRATE (gm)
♥	Chocolate Shake	16 oz.	445	77
♥ 🅱	**Colombo Yogurt Shakes** Chocolate Chip Regular Shake	11.5 oz.	480	57
♥ 🅱	Chocolate Covered Cherry Shake	12.5 oz.	540	72
♥ 🅱	Mint Chocolate Chip Regular Shake	12.5 oz.	570	80
♥ 🅱	Buckeye/Peanut Butter Kiss Shake	12.5 oz.	660	63

🅱 = More than 2 fat exchanges per serving

PROTEIN (gm)	FAT (gm)	SAT. FAT (gm)	CHOLES- TEROL (mg)	SODIUM (mg)	Exchanges
9	4	NA	0	160	4 starch
9	4	NA	0	160	4 starch, 1 fat
9	4	NA	0	160	4 starch, 1 fat
9	1	NA	0	160	4 starch
9	7	NA	7	200	4 starch, 1 fat
9	12	8	35	248	
10	23	NA	0	150	
10	23	NA	0	200	
10	23	NA	0	170	
15	41	NA	1	300	

☨ = More than 800 milligrams sodium   ♥ = High amounts of sugar

	Products	SERVING SIZE	CALORIES	CARBO-HYDRATE (gm)
	SUBWAY			
	Subs			
✳	Cold Cut Comb Sub	6 inch	427	41
▮ ✳	Spicy Italian Sub	6 inch	522	41
▮ ✳	BMT Sub	6 inch	491	41
✳	Subway Club Sub	6 inch	346	42
▮	Tuna Sub	6 inch	552	41
▮ ✳	Seafood & Crab Sub	6 inch	493	47
✳	Seafood & Lobster Sub	6 inch	472	47
✳	Meatball Sub	6 inch	458	48
	Steak & Cheese Sub	6 inch	383	42
✳	Turkey Breast Sub	6 inch	322	41
✳	Roast Beef Sub	6 inch	345	42

▮ = More than 2 fat exchanges per serving

PROTEIN (gm)	FAT (gm)	SAT. FAT (gm)	CHOLES- TEROL (mg)	SODIUM (mg)	Exchanges
23	20	6	80	1110	3 starch, 2 med. fat meat, 1 fat
21	32	12	70	1510	3 starch, 2 med. fat meat, 3 fat
22	28	10	70	1570	3 starch, 2 med. fat meat, 3 fat
23	11	4	40	1360	3 starch, 2 med. fat meat
18	36	7	40	750	3 starch, 2 med. fat meat, 4 fat
15	28	6	30	980	3 starch, 2 med. fat meat, 3 fat
14	26	5	30	1040	3 starch, 2 med. fat meat, 2 fat
21	22	8	40	1010	3 starch, 2 med. fat meat, 2 fat
22	16	6	40	790	3 starch, 2 med. fat meat
20	10	3	30	1230	3 starch, 2 lean meat
21	12	4	40	1140	3 starch, 2 lean meat

♈ = More than 800 milligrams sodium   ♟ = High amounts of sugar

Products	SERVING SIZE	CALORIES	CARBO-HYDRATE (gm)
ⵏ Ham & Cheese Sub	6 inch	322	41
Veggies & Cheese Sub	6 inch	268	41

Salads

Products	SERVING SIZE	CALORIES	CARBO-HYDRATE (gm)
▯ ⵏ Cold Cut Combo Salad	Small	305	12
▯ ⵏ Cold Cut Combo Salad	Regular	506	14
▯ ⵏ Spicy Italian Salad	Small	400	12
▯ ⵏ Spicy Italian Salad	Regular	696	14
▯ ⵏ BMT Salad	Small	369	12
▯ ⵏ BMT Salad	Regular	635	14
ⵏ Subway Club Salad	Small	225	12
ⵏ Subway Club Salad	Regular	346	14
▯ Tuna Salad	Small	430	12

▯ = More than 2 fat exchanges per serving

PROTEIN (gm)	FAT (gm)	SAT. FAT (gm)	CHOLES-TEROL (mg)	SODIUM (mg)	Exchanges
19	9	3	40	1220	3 starch, 2 lean meat
10	9	3	10	540	3 starch, ½ med. fat meat
18	25	6	80	910	2 vegetable, 2 med. fat meat, 3 fat
33	37	11	170	1820	2 vegetable, 4 med. fat meat, 4 fat
16	33	12	70	1140	2 vegetable, 2 med. fat meat, 5 fat
29	60	22	140	2280	2 vegetable, 4 med. fat meat, 8 fat
17	29	10	70	1200	2 vegetable, 2 med. fat meat, 4 fat
31	52	23	130	2400	2 vegetable, 4 med. fat meat, 6 fat
18	13	3	40	990	2 vegetable, 2 med. fat meat, 1 fat
32	19	6	80	1980	2 vegetable, 4 med. fat meat
13	38	6	40	380	2 vegetable, 2 med. fat meat, 5 fat

☂ = More than 800 milligrams sodium   ♥ = High amounts of sugar

Products	SERVING SIZE	CALORIES	CARBO-HYDRATE (gm)
▤ Tuna Salad	Regular	756	12
▤ Seafood & Crab Salad	Small	371	18
▤ ☂ Seafood & Crab Salad	Regular	639	25
▤ Seafood & Lobster Salad	Small	351	18
▤ ☂ Seafood & Lobster Salad	Regular	597	26
☂ Turkey Breast Salad	Small	201	12
☂ Turkey Breast Salad	Regular	297	14
Roast Beef Salad	Small	222	13
☂ Roast Beef Salad	Regular	340	15
☂ Ham & Cheese Salad	Small	200	11
☂ Ham & Cheese Salad	Regular	296	12
Veggies & Cheese Salad	Regular	188	12

▤ = More than 2 fat exchanges per serving

PROTEIN (gm)	FAT (gm)	SAT. FAT (gm)	CHOLES-TEROL (mg)	SODIUM (mg)	Exchanges
23	68	12	90	760	2 vegetable, 3 med. fat meat, 10 fat
10	30	5	30	610	2 vegetable, 1 med. fat meat, 5 fat
16	53	10	60	1230	2 vegetable, 1 starch, 2 med. fat meat, 8 fat
9	28	5	30	670	2 vegetable, 1 med. fat meat, 5 fat
15	49	9	60	1340	2 vegetable, 1 starch, 2 med. fat meat, 7 fat
15	11	3	30	860	2 vegetable, 2 med. fat meat
27	16	5	70	1720	2 vegetable, 3 med. fat meat
16	10	4	40	780	2 vegetable, 2 med. fat meat
29	20	7	80	1550	2 vegetable, 4 med. fat meat
14	12	3	40	860	2 vegetable, 2 med. fat meat
25	18	6	70	1710	2 vegetable, 3 med. fat meat, 1 fat
7	14	4	20	340	2 vegetable, ½ med. fat meat, 2 fat

⍭ = More than 800 milligrams sodium   ♥ = High amounts of sugar

Products	SERVING SIZE	CALORIES	CARBO-HYDRATE (gm)
Salad Dressings			
🄱 Blue Cheese	2 oz.	322	14
🄱 Thousand Island	2 oz.	252	10
🄱 Lite-Italian	2 oz.	23	4
🄱 French	2 oz.	264	20
🄱 Creamy Italian	2 oz.	256	5

TACO BELL

Specialties

🍗 Bean Burrito	1 (6.7 OZ.)	359	54
🍗 Beef Burrito	1 (6.7 OZ.)	402	38
🍗 Double Beef Burrito Supreme	1 (9 OZ.)	451	40
Tostada	1 (5.5 OZ.)	243	28
Beefy Tostada	1 (7 OZ.)	322	22
Beef Meximelt	1 (3.7 oz.)	266	19
Chicken Meximelt	1 (3.8 oz.)	257	19

🄱 = More than 2 fat exchanges per serving

PROTEIN (gm)	FAT (gm)	SAT. FAT (gm)	CHOLES-TEROL (mg)	SODIUM (mg)	Exchanges
2	29	5	274	578	1 starch, 6 fat
1	24	4	186	514	½ starch, 5 fat
1	1	tr	10	952	Free
tr	20	3	1	462	1 starch, 4 fat
tr	26	4	119	548	5 fat
13	11	5	13	922	3½ starch, 1 med. fat meat, 1 fat
22	17	8	59	993	2½ starch, 2 med. fat meat, 1 fat
23	22	10	59	928	3 starch, 2 med. fat meat, 2 fat
10	11	5	18	670	2 starch, 1 med. fat meat, 1 fat
15	20	10	40	764	1½ starch, 1½ med. fat meat, 2 fat
13	15	8	38	689	1 starch, 1½ med. fat meat, 2 fat
14	15	7	48	779	1 starch, 1½ med. fat meat, 2 fat

☂ = More than 800 milligrams sodium   ♣ = High amounts of sugar

	Products	SERVING SIZE	CALORIES	CARBO-HYDRATE (gm)
⚕	Bellbeefer	1 (6.2 oz.)	312	32
⚕	Chicken Burrito	1 (6 oz.)	334	38
⚕	Burrito Supreme	1 (8.7 oz.)	422	46
⚕	Combination Burrito	1 (6.7 oz.)	380	46
⚕	Enchirito	1 (7.5 oz.)	382	30
	Taco	1 (2.75 oz.)	184	11
	Chicken Soft Taco	1 (3.7 oz.)	213	19
◳ ⚕	Taco Light Platter	1 (17 oz.)	1062	97
◳ ⚕	Burrito Supreme Platter	1 (16 oz.)	774	76
	Cheesarito	1 (4 oz.)	312	37
◳ ⚕	Mexican Pizza	1 (9.5 oz.)	714	43
◳ ⚕	Taco Bellgrande Platter	1 (17 oz.)	1002	99

◳ = More than 2 fat exchanges per serving

PROTEIN (gm)	FAT (gm)	SAT. FAT (gm)	CHOLES- TEROL (mg)	SODIUM (mg)	Exchanges
16	13	6	39	855	2 starch, 1½ med. fat meat, 1 fat
17	12	4	52	880	2½ starch, 2 med. fat meat
17	19	9	35	952	3 starch, 1½ med. fat meat, 2 fat
17	14	6	36	957	3 starch, 1½ med. fat meat, 1 fat
21	20	10	56	1260	2 starch, 2 med. fat meat, 2 fat
10	11	4	32	274	1 starch, 2 lean meat
14	10	4	52	615	1 starch, 2 med. fat meat
38	58	34	82	2068	6 starch, 3 med. fat meat, 8 fat
35	37	19	79	1920	5 starch, 3 med. meat, 4 fat
12	13	7	29	451	2 starch, 1 med. meat, 2 fat
28	48	31	81	1364	3 starch, 3 med. fat meat, 6 fat
37	51	29	80	1962	6½ starch, 3 med. fat meat, 6 fat

☂ = More than 800 milligrams sodium   ♥ = High amounts of sugar

Products	SERVING SIZE	CALORIES	CARBO-HYDRATE (gm)
Pintos & Cheese	1 order (4.5 oz.)	194	19
𐌁 Nachos	1 order (3.7 oz.)	346	37
𐌁 ✳ Nachos Bellgrande	1 order (10 oz.)	649	61
𐌁 Taco Bellgrande	1 (6 oz.)	351	20
𐌁 Taco Light	1 (6 oz.)	411	18
Soft Taco	1 (3.25 oz.)	228	18
Fajita Steak Taco	1 (5 oz.)	235	20
Fajita Steak Taco w/Sour Cream	1 (5.75 oz.)	281	21
Fajita Steak Taco w/Guacamole	1 (5.75 oz.)	269	23
Chicken Fajita	1 (4.75 oz.)	226	20
𐌁 Cinnamon Crisps	1 order (1.6 oz.)	266	20

Condiments

Taco Sauce	1 packet	2	tr

𐌁 = More than 2 fat exchanges per serving

PROTEIN (gm)	FAT (gm)	SAT. FAT (gm)	CHOLES-TEROL (mg)	SODIUM (mg)	Exchanges
9	10	5	19	733	1 starch, 1 med. fat meat, 1 fat
7	18	6	9	399	2½ starch, 4 fat
22	35	12	36	997	4 starch, 2 med. fat meat, 6 fat
18	22	13	55	470	1 starch, 2 med. fat meat, 3 fat
19	29	18	57	575	1 starch, 2 med. fat meat, 4 fat
12	12	5	32	516	1 starch, 1½ med. fat meat, 1 fat
15	11	5	14	507	1 starch, 2 med. fat meat
15	15	7	14	507	1 starch, 2 med. fat meat, 1 fat
15	13	5	14	620	1 starch, 2 med. fat meat, 1 fat
14	10	4	44	619	1 starch, 2 med. fat meat
3	16	13	2	122	2 starch, 3 fat
tr	tr	0	0	126	Free

☀ = More than 800 milligrams sodium　　♥ = High amounts of sugar

	Products	SERVING SIZE	CALORIES	CARBO-HYDRATE (gm)
	Salsa	1 packet (.35 oz.)	18	4
▤	Ranch Dressing	1 packet (2.6 oz.)	236	1
	Guacamole	1 serving (.75 oz.)	34	3

Salads

	Products	SERVING SIZE	CALORIES	CARBO-HYDRATE (gm)
▤ ☀	Taco Salad w/out Beans	1 (18 oz.)	822	47
▤ ☀	Taco Salad w/out Salsa	1 (18 oz.)	931	60
▤ ☀	Taco Salad with Ranch Dressing	1 (20 oz.)	1167	61
▤ ☀	Seafood Salad w/Ranch Dressing	1 (15 oz.)	884	49
	Seafood Salad w/out Dressing/ Shell	1 (10 oz.)	217	12
▤ ☀	Seafood Salad w/out Dressing	1 (13 oz.)	648	47
▤ ☀	Taco Salad w/Salsa	1 (21 oz.)	949	63
▤ ☀	Taco Salad w/out Shell	1 (18.7 oz.)	502	26

▤ = More than 2 fat exchanges per serving

PROTEIN (gm)	FAT (gm)	SAT. FAT (gm)	CHOLES-TEROL (mg)	SODIUM (mg)	Exchanges
1	tr	0	0	376	Free
2	25	5	35	571	5 fat
tr	2	tr	0	113	½ fat
31	57	38	81	1368	3 starch, 3 med. fat meat, 8 fat
35	62	40	85	1387	4 starch, 3½ med. fat meat, 8 fat
37	87	45	121	1959	4 starch, 3½ med. fat meat, 13 fat
25	66	34	117	1489	3 starch, 3 med. fat meat, 10 fat
18	11	6	81	693	1 starch, 2 med. fat meat
24	42	30	82	917	3 starch, 2 med. fat meat, 6 fat
36	62	40	86	1763	4 starch, 4 med. fat meat, 8 fat
29	31	14	80	1056	2 starch, 3 med. fat meat, 3 fat

☂ = More than 800 milligrams sodium   ♥ = High amounts of sugar

Products	SERVING SIZE	CALORIES	CARBO-HYDRATE (gm)
☨ Taco Salad w/Salsa, w/out Shell	1 (18.7 oz.)	520	30

WENDY'S

Sandwiches

Single Hamburger on Bun	1 (4.7 oz.)	350	31
☨ Single with Everything	1 (7.7 oz.)	440	36
Double Hamburger on bun	1 (7 oz.)	560	26
☨ Big Classic on Kaiser Bun	1 (8.9 oz.)	480	44
Double w/Cheese	1 (7.8 oz.)	620	26
Bacon Cheeseburger	1 (5.3 oz.)	440	26
� ☨ Country Fried Steak	1 (5.4 oz.)	460	45
Fish Sandwich	1 (6.4 oz.)	460	42
Grilled Chicken Sandwich	1 (6.25 oz.)	290	35

𝐁 = More than 2 fat exchanges per serving

PROTEIN (gm)	FAT (gm)	SAT. FAT (gm)	CHOLES-TEROL (mg)	SODIUM (mg)	Exchanges
31	31	14	80	1431	2 starch, 4 med. fat meat, 2 fat
25	15	6	70	510	2 starch, 3 med. fat meat
26	23	7	75	850	2 starch, 1 vegetable 3 med. fat meat, 1 fat
44	30	11	150	465	2 starch, 6 med. fat meat
27	23	7	75	850	3 starch, 3 med. fat meat, 1 fat
48	36	15	165	760	2 starch, 6 med. fat meat, 1 fat
30	24	20	95	680	2 starch, 3 med. fat meat, 2 fat
15	26	7	35	880	3 starch, 1 med. fat meat, 4 fat
18	25	5	55	780	3 starch, 2 med. fat meat, 2 fat
24	7	1	60	360	2 starch, 1 vegetable, 2 lean meat

☂ = More than 800 milligrams sodium   ♣ = High amounts of sugar

Products	SERVING SIZE	CALORIES	CARBO-HYDRATE (gm)
Breaded Chicken Sandwich	1 (7.3 oz.)	450	44
Chicken Club Sandwich	1 (7.75 oz.)	520	44
Jr. Hamburger	(4 oz.)	270	34
Jr. Cheeseburger	1 (4.5 oz.)	320	34
▤ Jr. Bacon Cheeseburger	1 (6 oz.)	440	33
Jr. Cheeseburger Deluxe	1 (6.3 oz.)	390	36
Hamburger, Kids' Meal	1 (4 oz.)	270	33
Cheeseburger, Kids' Meal	1 (4.3 oz.)	310	33
Sandwich Components ¼ lb. Hamburger Patty	1 (2.6 oz.)	190	tr
American Cheese Slice	1 slice	70	tr
Bacon	1 strip	30	tr
Ketchup	1 tsp.	7	2
Lettuce	1 leaf	2	tr

▤ = More than 2 fat exchanges per serving

PROTEIN (gm)	FAT (gm)	SAT. FAT (gm)	CHOLES- TEROL (mg)	SODIUM (mg)	Exchanges
26	20	4	60	740	3 starch, 2 med. fat meat, 2 fat
30	25	6	75	980	3 starch, 3 med. fat meat, 2 fat
15	9	3	35	590	2 starch, 1½ med. fat meat
18	13	5	45	760	2 starch, 2 med. fat meat
22	25	8	65	330	2 starch, 2 med. fat meat, 3 fat
18	20	7	50	320	2 starch, 2 vegetable, 2 med. fat meat, 2 fat
15	9	3	35	210	2 starch, 1½ med. fat meat
18	13	5	45	760	2 starch, 2 med. fat meat
19	12	5	70	220	3 med. fat meat
4	6	4	15	260	1 med. fat meat
2	2	1	5	125	1 fat
tr	tr	tr	0	75	Free
tr	tr	tr	0	tr	Free

🖣 = More than 800 milligrams sodium   ♥ = High amounts of sugar

Products	SERVING SIZE	CALORIES	CARBO-HYDRATE (gm)
Mayonnaise	2 tsp.	93	tr
Mustard	½ tsp.	4	tr
Onion	4 rings	2	tr
Dill Pickles	4 slices	2	tr
Tomatoes	1 slice	6	1
Red. Cal. Honey Mustard	1 tsp.	25	2
⊟ Tartar Sauce	1 Tbsp.	130	tr
Baked Potato			
Plain	1 (10 oz.)	300	69
⊼ Bacon & Cheese	1 (13.4 oz.)	510	75
Broccoli & Cheese	1 (14.5 oz.)	450	77
⊟ Cheese	1 (13.5 oz.)	550	74
Chili & Cheese	1 (15.5 oz.)	600	80
Sour Cream & Chives	1 (11 oz.)	370	71
Sour Cream	1 pkt.	60	1

⊟ = More than 2 fat exchanges per serving

PROTEIN (gm)	FAT (gm)	SAT. FAT (gm)	CHOLES-TEROL (mg)	SODIUM (mg)	Exchanges
tr	10	1	8	60	2 fats
tr	tr	tr	0	65	Free
tr	tr	tr	0	tr	Free
tr	tr	tr	0	160	Free
tr	tr	tr	0	tr	Free
tr	2	tr	0	45	Free
tr	14	2	15	115	3 fat
6	tr	tr	0	20	4 starch
17	17	4	15	1170	5 starch, 1 med. fat meat, 2 fat
9	14	2	0	450	5 starch, 2 fat
14	24	8	30	640	5 starch, 1 med. fat meat, 3 fat
21	25	9	45	740	5 starch, 2 med. fat meat, 2 fat
8	6	4	15	35	4½ starch, 1 fat
1	6	4	15	15	1 fat

� = More than 800 milligrams sodium   ♥ = High amounts of sugar

Products	SERVING SIZE	CALORIES	CARBO-HYDRATE (gm)
French Fries, Nuggets, and Chili			
Small	3.2 oz.	240	33
⨷ Medium	4.8 oz.	360	50
⨷ Biggie	6 oz.	450	62
Chicken Nuggets	6 pieces	280	12
Barbecue Sauce	1 pkt.	50	11
Sweet & Sour Sauce	1 pkt.	45	11
Sweet Mustard	1 pkt.	50	9
Chili	Small (8 oz.)	190	21
ⵈ Chili	Large (12 oz.)	290	31
Cheddar Cheese,	2 Tbsp. shredded	70	1
Saltine Crackers	6	75	12
Salads			
Caesar Side Salad	1 (4.5 oz.)	160	18

⨷ = More than 2 fat exchanges per serving

PROTEIN (gm)	FAT (gm)	SAT. FAT (gm)	CHOLES-TEROL (mg)	SODIUM (mg)	Exchanges
3	12	2	0	150	2 starch, 2 fat
5	17	4	0	220	3 starch, 3 fat
6	22	5	0	280	4 starch, 4 fat
14	20	5	50	600	1 starch, 2 med. fat meat, 1 fat
1	0	0	0	100	1 starch or fruit
1	tr	0	0	55	1 fruit
1	1	tr	0	140	1 fruit
19	6	2	40	670	1½ starch, 2 lean meat
28	9	4	60	1000	2 starch, 3 lean meat
4	6	4	20	120	1 med. fat meat
2	3	tr	0	240	1 starch
10	6	1	10	700	3 vegetable or 1 starch, ½ med. fat meat, 1 fat

� = More than 800 milligrams sodium   ♥ = High amounts of sugar

Products	SERVING SIZE	CALORIES	CARBO-HYDRATE (gm)
Deluxe Garden Salad	1 (9.6 oz.)	110	9
⚹ Taco Salad	1 (18 oz.)	640	70
Taco Sauce	1 pkg.	10	tr
Grilled Chicken Salad	1 (12 oz.)	200	9
Side Salad	1 (6.6 oz.)	60	4
Breadstick	1 (1.5 oz.)	130	24

Garden Spot Salad Bar

Lettuce, Iceberg or Romaine	3 cup	29	6
	1 cup	10	2
Alfalfa Sprouts	½ cup	4	1
Applesauce	2 Tbsp.	30	8
Bacon Bits	2 Tbsp.	45	1
Bread Sticks	4	56	8
Broccoli	¼ cup	4	1
Cantaloupe, sliced	1 piece	16	4
Carrots	¼ cup	6	2
Cauliflower	¼ cup	4	1

目 = More than 2 fat exchanges per serving

PROTEIN (gm)	FAT (gm)	SAT. FAT (gm)	CHOLES- TEROL (mg)	SODIUM (mg)	Exchanges
7	5	1	0	380	2 vegetable, 1 fat
34	30	12	80	960	2 vegetable, 4 starch, 3 med. fat meat, 2 fat
tr	tr	0	0	105	Free
25	8	1	55	690	2 vegetable, 3 lean meat
3	tr	0	0	200	1 vegetable, 1 fat
4	3	1	5	250	1½ starch
2	tr	tr	0	20	1 vegetable
1	tr	tr	0	5	Free
1	tr	tr	0	tr	Free
tr	tr	tr	0	tr	½ fruit
5	2	1	5	430	½ med. fat meat
1	1	tr	0	100	½ starch
tr	tr	tr	0	tr	Free
tr	tr	tr	0	tr	Free
tr	tr	tr	0	5	Free
tr	tr	tr	0	tr	Free

☛ = More than 800 milligrams sodium   ♥ = High amounts of sugar

Products	SERVING SIZE	CALORIES	CARBO-HYDRATE (gm)
Cheddar Chips	2 Tbsp.	70	5
Cheese, shredded	2 Tbsp.	50	1
Chicken Salad	2 Tbsp.	70	2
Chow Mein Noodles	¼ cup	35	4
California Cole Slaw	2 Tbsp.	45	5
Cottage Cheese	1 Tbsp.	30	1
Croutons	¼ cup	30	8
Cucumbers	2 slices	2	tr
Eggs, hard cooked	2 Tbsp.	40	tr
Garbanzo Beans	2 Tbsp.	45	7
Green Peas	2 Tbsp.	20	3
Green Pepper	2 pieces	2	1
Honeydew Melon, sliced	1 piece	18	5
Jalapeno Peppers	1 Tbsp.	2	1
Mushrooms	¼ cup	14	1
Olives, black	2 Tbsp.	16	1
Orange, sectioned	1 piece	14	4
Pasta Salad	2 Tbsp.	80	11
Peaches, sliced	1 piece	20	6

ᗺ = More than 2 fat exchanges per serving

PROTEIN (gm)	FAT (gm)	SAT. FAT (gm)	CHOLES-TEROL (mg)	SODIUM (mg)	Exchanges
1	5	1	0	170	1 fat
4	4	1	0	280	½ med. fat meat
4	5	1	0	135	1 med. fat meat
1	2	tr	0	55	Free
tr	3	tr	5	60	1 vegetable, 1 fat
4	1	1	5	125	½ lean meat
2	2	tr	NA	130	½ starch
tr	tr	tr	0	tr	Free
3	3	1	120	30	½ med. fat meat
2	1	tr	0	tr	½ starch
1	tr	tr	0	25	Free
tr	tr	tr	0	tr	Free
tr	tr	tr	0	5	Free
tr	tr	tr	0	160	Free
tr	tr	tr	0	tr	Free
tr	1	tr	0	120	Free
tr	tr	tr	0	0	Free
2	4	NA	5	115	½ starch, 1 fat
tr	tr	tr	0	tr	Free

� = More than 800 milligrams sodium   ♥ = High amounts of sugar

Products	SERVING SIZE	CALORIES	CARBO-HYDRATE (gm)
Pepperoni, sliced	6 pieces	30	tr
Pineapple, chunked	4 piece	20	5
Potato Salad	2 Tbsp.	70	4
♥ Pudding, Chocolate or Vanilla	¼ cup	80	10
Red Onions	3 rings	4	1
Seafood Salad	¼ cup	70	5
Strawberries	1 each	8	2
♥ Strawberry Banana Dessert	¼ cup	110	28
Sunflower Seeds & Raisins	2 Tbsp.	80	4
Three Bean Salad	2 Tbsp.	30	6
Tomato, wedged	1 piece	6	1
Tuna Salad	2 Tbsp.	100	4
Turkey Ham, diced	2 Tbsp.	30	1
Watermelon, wedged	1 piece	20	4

Salad Dressings (1 ladle equals 2 tablespoons)

Products	SERVING SIZE	CALORIES	CARBO-HYDRATE (gm)
ᗷ Bleu Cheese	2 Tbsp.	180	tr
Celery Seed	2 Tbsp.	130	6

ᗷ = More than 2 fat exchanges per serving

PROTEIN (gm)	FAT (gm)	SAT. FAT (gm)	CHOLES- TEROL (mg)	SODIUM (mg)	Exchanges
1	3	1	5	95	½ fat
tr	tr	tr	0	tr	Free
tr	5	NA	NA	170	1 vegetable, 1 fat
1	3	NA	0	60	1 starch
tr	tr	tr	0	tr	Free
3	4	1	0	300	½ med. fat meat
tr	tr	tr	0	tr	Free
1	tr	tr	0	tr	2 fruit
3	6	NA	0	tr	½ fruit, 1 fat
1	tr	tr	NA	10	1 vegetable
tr	tr	tr	0	tr	Free
7	6	1	0	270	1 med. fat meat
4	12	tr	15	210	½ lean meat
tr	tr	tr	0	tr	½ fruit
1	19	4	20	200	3 fat
tr	11	2	5	120	2 fat

🍴 = More than 800 milligrams sodium   🍬 = High amounts of sugar

Products	SERVING SIZE	CALORIES	CARBO-HYDRATE (gm)
French	2 Tbsp.	120	6
French, Sweet Red	2 Tbsp.	130	9
Hidden Valley Ranch	2 Tbsp.	100	1
⊟ Italian Caesar	2 Tbsp.	150	1
Italian, Golden	2 Tbsp.	90	6
Red. Cal. Bacon & Tomato	2 Tbsp.	90	5
Red. Cal. Italian	2 Tbsp.	50	3
⊟ Salad Oil	1 Tbsp.	120	0
⊟ Thousand Island	2 Tbsp.	130	3
Wine Vinegar	1 Tbsp.	2	tr

Mexican Fiesta

Cheese Sauce	¼ cup	40	5
Picante Sauce	2 Tbsp.	10	2
Refried Beans	¼ cup	70	9
Spanish Rice	¼ cup	60	11
Sour Topping	2 Tbsp.	45	1
Taco Chips	8 each	160	25
Taco Meat	2 Tbsp.	80	2
Taco Sauce	2 Tbsp.	12	2

⊟ = More than 2 fat exchanges per serving

PROTEIN (gm)	FAT (gm)	SAT. FAT (gm)	CHOLES- TEROL (mg)	SODIUM (mg)	Exchanges
tr	10	2	0	330	2 fat
tr	10	2	0	230	2 fat
1	10	2	10	220	2 fat
1	16	3	10	260	3 fat
tr	7	1	0	460	1½ fat
tr	7	1	0	350	1½ fat
tr	4	1	0	340	1 fat
0	14	2	0	0	3 fat
tr	13	2	15	200	3 fat
tr	tr	tr	0	tr	Free
1	2	tr	0	310	½ fat
tr	tr	tr	NA	tr	Free
3	2	1	0	200	1 starch
1	1	tr	NA	390	1 starch
1	4	NA	0	25	1 fat
3	6	1	NA	15	1½ starch, 1 fat
7	4	1	15	200	1 med. fat meat
tr	tr	tr	NA	110	Free

ᵀ = More than 800 milligrams sodium   ♥ = High amounts of sugar

Products	SERVING SIZE	CALORIES	CARBO-HYDRATE (gm)
Taco Shells	2 each	100	12
Tortilla, Flour	1 each	100	18

Pasta Salad Bar

Alfredo Sauce	¼ cup	30	4
Fettucini	½ cup	66	18
Garlic Toast	2 piece	140	18
Macaroni & Cheese	½ cup	130	14
Pasta Medley	½ cup	60	8
Red Peppers, crushed	1 Tbsp.	20	3
Roma/Parm Blend, grated	2 Tbsp.	70	5
Rotini	½ cup	90	15
Spaghetti Sauce	¼ cup	30	6
Spaghetti Meat Sauce	¼ cup	45	6

OCCASIONAL USE

☕ Frosty Dairy Dessert	Small (12 oz.)	340	57
☕ Chocolate Chip Cookie	1 each	280	39

☕ = More than 2 fat exchanges per serving

PROTEIN (gm)	FAT (gm)	SAT. FAT (gm)	CHOLES- TEROL (mg)	SODIUM (mg)	Exchanges
2	6	NA	NA	90	1 starch, 1 fat
3	3	NA	NA	210	1 starch, 1 fat
1	1	tr	0	260	1 vegetable
5	4	1	10	tr	1 starch
4	6	2	0	40	1 starch, 1 fat
4	6	3	5	320	1 starch, 1 fat
2	2	tr	NA	tr	½ starch
1	1	tr	0	tr	Free
3	3	2	10	250	1 med. fat meat
3	2	tr	NA	NA	1 starch
1	tr	tr	0	340	1 vegetable
3	1	1	5	230	1 vegetable
9	10	5	40	200	4 starch, 2 fat
3	13	4	15	260	2½ starch, 2 fat

🦷 = More than 800 milligrams sodium   🍬 = High amounts of sugar

Products	SERVING SIZE	CALORIES	CARBO-HYDRATE (gm)
NOT RECOMMENDED FOR USE			
♥ Frosty Dairy Dessert	Medium (16 oz.)	460	76
♥ Frosty Dairy Dessert	Large (20 oz.)	570	95

PROTEIN (gm)	FAT (gm)	SAT. FAT (gm)	CHOLES- TEROL (mg)	SODIUM (mg)	Exchanges
12	13	7	55	260	
15	17	9	70	330	

The Joy of Snacks by Nancy Cooper, R.D. Offers more than 200 delicious recipes and nutrition information for hearty snacks, including sandwiches, appetizers, soups, spreads, cookies, muffins, and treats especially for kids. The book also suggests guidelines for selecting convenience snacks and interpreting information on food labels.

    004086,   ISBN 0-937721-82-4 $12.95

The Healthy Eater's Guide to Family & Chain Restaurants by Hope S. Warshaw, M.M.Sc., R.D. Here's the only guide that tells you how to eat healthier in over 100 of America's most popular family and chain restaurants. It offers complete and up-to-date nutrition information and suggests which items to choose and avoid.

    004214,   ISBN 1-56561-017-2 $9.95

Fight Fat & Win by Elaine Moquette-Magee, M.P.H., R.D. This breakthrough book explains how to easily lower the fat in everything you eat from fast food and common restaurants to quick meals at home, simply by making smarter choices.

    004244   ISBN 1-56561-047-4 $9.95

How Should I Feed My Child? From Pregnancy to Preschool by Sandra Nissenberg, M.S., R.D., Margaret Bogle, Ph.D., R.D., Edna Langholz, M.S., R.D., and Audrey Wright, M.S., R.D. Addressing real issues and parents' most common concerns, this guide tells how to start your child off to a lifetime of good eating habits. Includes over 50 recipes.

"From four nutrition experts with impressive credentials, the book offers easy-to-read, practical advice."
-USA Today
* A Doubleday Health Book Club Selection

    004232,   ISBN 1-56561-035-0 $12.95

200 Kid-Tested Ways to Lower the Fat in Your Child's Favorite Foods by Elaine Moquette-Magee, M.P.H., R.D. For the first time ever, here's a much needed and asked for guide that gives easy, step-by-step instructions on cutting the fat in the most popular brand name and homemade foods kids eat every day—without them even noticing.
* A Doubleday Health Book Club Selection
    004231,   ISBN 1-56561-034-2 $12.95

All-American Low-Fat Meals in Minutes by M.J. Smith, M.A., R.D., L.D. Filled with tantalizing recipes and valuable tips, this cookbook makes great-tasting, low-fat foods a snap for holidays, special occasions, or everyday. Most recipes take only minutes to prepare.
    004079,   ISBN 0-937721-73-5 $12.95

60 Days of Low-Fat, Low-Cost Meals in Minutes by M.J. Smith, R.D., L.D., M.A. Following the path of the best-seller *All American Low-Fat Meals in Minutes,* here are more than 150 quick and sumptuous recipes complete with the latest exchange values and nutrition facts for lowering calories, fat, salt, and cholesterol. This book contains complete menus for 60 days and recipes that use ingredients found in virtually any grocery store—most for a total cost of less than $10.
    004205,   ISBN 1-56561-010-5 $12.95

The Guiltless Gourmet by Judy Gilliard and Joy Kirkpatrick, R.D. A perfect fusion of sound nutrition and creative cooking, this book is loaded with delicious recipes high in flavor and low in fat, sugar, calories, cholesterol, and salt.
    004021,   ISBN 0-937721-23-9 $9.95

The Guiltless Gourmet Goes Ethnic by Judy Gilliard and Joy Kirkpatrick, R.D. More than a cookbook, this sequel to *The Guiltless*

Gourmet shows how easy it is to lower the sugar, calories, sodium, and fat in your favorite ethnic dishes—without sacrificing taste.

    004072,   ISBN 0-937721-68-9 $11.95

European Cuisine from the Guiltless Gourmet by Judy Gilliard and Joy Kirkpatrick, R.D. This book shows you how to lower the sugar, salt, cholesterol, total fat, and calories in delicious Greek, English, German, Russian, and Scandinavian dishes. Plus, it features complete nutrition information and the latest exchange values.

    004085,   ISBN 0-937721-81-6 $11.95

Beyond Alfalfa Sprouts & Cheese: The Healthy Meatless Cookbook by Judy Gilliard and Joy Kirkpatrick, R.D., includes creative and savory meatless dishes using ingredients found in just about every grocery store. It also contains helpful cooking tips, complete nutrition information, and the latest exchange values.

004218,   ISBN 1-56561-020-2 $12.95

One Year of Healthy, Hearty, & Simple One-Dish Meals by Pam Spaude and Jan Owan-McMenamin, R.D., is a collection of 365 easy-to-make healthy and tasty family favorites and unique creations that are meals in themselves. Most of the dishes take under 30 minutes to prepare.

    004217,   ISBN 1-56561-019-9 $12.95

Let Them Eat Cake by Virginia N. White with Rosa A. Mo, R.D. If you're looking for delicious and healthy pies, cookies, puddings, and cakes, this book will give you your just desserts. With easy, step-by-step instructions, this innovative cookbook features complete nutrition information, the latest exchange values, and tips on making your favorite snacks more healthful.

    004206,   ISBN 1-56561-011-3 $12.95

CHRONIMED Publishing
P.O. Box 47945
Minneapolis, MN 55447-9727

Circle the book (s) you would like sent. Enclosed is $_____.
(Please add $3.00 to this order to cover postage and handling.
Minnesota residents add 6.5% sales tax.) Send check or money order,
no cash or C.O.D.'s. Prices are subject to change without notice.

Name _____

Address _____

City _____

State_____Zip_____

Allow 4 to 6 weeks for delivery.
Quantity discounts available upon request.

Or order by phone: 1-800-848-2793,
612-546-1146 (Minneapolis/St. Paul metro area).
Please have your credit card number ready.